THE TOPKAPI SARAY MUSEUM

Costumes, Embroideries and other Textiles

The Topkapı Saray Museum

Costumes, Embroideries and other Textiles

translated, expanded and edited by
J. M. ROGERS
from the original Turkish by
HÜLYE TEZCAN *and* SELMA DELIBAŞ

A New York Graphic Society Book
Little, Brown and Company · Boston

Photographs by Banri Namikawa

Text and notes on the illustrations based on original material by Hülye Tezcan and Selma Delibaş, translated from the Turkish, edited and expanded by J. M. Rogers

This publication is adapted from and includes color plates first published in *Topkapı Sarayı Müzesi* (© 1980 Dentsu Incorporated, Tokyo) by the Topkapı Saray Museum Association, Tokyo, a subsidiary of Dentsu Incorporated

International Standard Book Number: 0-8212-1634-1
Library of Congress Catalog Card Number: 86-61004

First United States edition

New York Graphic Society books are published by Little, Brown and Company (Inc.)
Published simultaneously in Canada by Little, Brown & Company (Canada) Limited

Phototypeset in Great Britain
Text printed in Switzerland
Illustrations printed in Japan
Bound in Switzerland

Contents

Editor's note / *6*

Foreword / *7*

PART I: COSTUMES / *9*

1 The Collection of Sultans' and other Ottoman costumes and embroideries in the Topkapı Saray and their history / *11*

2 Silk textiles: geography and types / *15*

3 Dyes and dyestuffs / *18*

4 The silk industry: organization / *20*

5 Garments: Fashion, style and pattern / *25*

6 Some sources for the history of Ottoman textiles / *31*

7 Hierarchies and rank / *37*

8 Wool and mohair / *39*

9 The Ottoman fur trade / *42*

Costumes: Captions and notes to illustrations 1–85 / *47*

PART II: EMBROIDERIES / *157*

Turkish embroideries: historical documentation / *159*

Embroideries: Captions and notes to illustrations 86–121 / *169*

Bibliographical note / *211*

Concordance of illustrations / *213*

Index / *215*

Editor's note

The text of the present volume has been translated and adapted from the Turkish authors' original version (prepared, with editorial co-ordination by the late Kemal Çiğ, for the Japanese edition published in 1980); it has also been expanded by me for this edition, and many specific bibliographical citations have been added in the notes on the text at the end of individual chapters and in the descriptive notes following each section of illustrations. A list of titles of general interest is given in the Bibliographical note on p. 211.

Transliteration
Differences in the phonetic structure of Arabic, Persian and Turkish make absolute consistency in transliteration impossible. The standard system used for Arabic (*Encyclopaedia of Islam*, 2nd ed.) with a few modifications works, in the editor's view, well enough for Persian. But for Ottoman Turkish, to make it easy for the reader to consult primary sources, account has been taken of the modern romanized Turkish alphabet: since Ottoman contains a large proportion of Arabic and Persian words, the effect is inevitably occasionally bizarre. There is, regrettably, no simple solution. Place names, however, are given in their modern form, without diacriticals.

J.M.R.

Foreword

FROM the later fifteenth century until the Turkish revolution of 1924 the Topkapı Saray was one of the principal residences of the Ottoman Sultans. Prior to the capture of Constantinople by Meḥmed II in 1453, their capitals were Bursa and Edirne, which they continued to frequent seasonally. But after 1453 Constantinople, or Istanbul – cheerfully distorted by the seventeenth-century Ottoman historians to 'Islāmbol' (abounding in Islam) – was the seat of their empire.

The Great Palace of the Byzantine Emperors had disappeared centuries earlier and there was no large palace building standing which could readily be adapted to the imperial needs of Meḥmed the Conqueror. His first residence in Istanbul was the Eski Saray in the ruined Forum of Theodosius, between the Byzantine Forum Tauri and the markets going down to the Golden Horn, a site now occupied by Istanbul University. By the early 1470s, however, he had left this for the Acropolis of ancient Byzantium, a terrace dominating both the Sea of Marmara and the Golden Horn and enjoying views far up the Bosphorus. This was later to become known as the Topkapı Saray, the Palace of the Cannon Gate, and the Eski Saray was abandoned to concubines out of favour and pensioned palace servants. As well as being the Sultans' residence, with enormous kitchens, audience halls, grand reception rooms and separate quarters for the women, the complex of buildings was also, symbolically and in fact, the heart of an empire: its religious centre; the seat of the administration; the Treasury; and a vast storehouse of booty. It rapidly came to be a virtually self-sufficient entity, with mosques, schools, baths, Court workshops, gardens, libraries and prisons, and also included the Mint, Chancery (Divan), the Armoury (in the Byzantine church of Haghia Eirene in the first courtyard of the palace), and a shrine (the Hırka-i Saadet Dairesi) to house the relics brought back from Mecca and Medina by Selīm I (1512–20) – the whole being administered with the help of an enormous resident or semi-resident staff of servants, male and female attendants, guards, physicians, craftsmen and minor officials of all sorts.

While many of the first pavilions, as was Ottoman practice, were wooden and have since disappeared the Hazine (Treasury, so-called because it was used to house the revenues of Egypt under Selīm I), built in 873/1468–9 on a high basement, was of cut stone. Like the three grand gateways of the Palace, it was there to impress, to give a suitable architectural setting for the ceremonies and splendours of the Sultan and his Court. The buildings added in the sixteenth and seventeenth centuries – with their rich marbles, tile-panels, inlaid wooden shutters, doors and panelling and their imposing calligraphy – skilfully combine strength and delicacy. Yet although each of them is the product of a personal whim or fantasy, the ensemble has a unity which makes the Topkapı one of the most striking surviving palaces of Europe or Asia. Parts of it fell into decay or were torn down by later Sultans who wished for buildings more in the current style; much also was destroyed by periodic fires. Since the Topkapı Saray became a museum in 1924, however, a programme of careful restoration has made it accessible to the public, some parts of it after centuries of neglect. The buildings, and their gardens and fountains, are thus now a living environment for the fabulously rich collections the museum contains and give the Topkapı Saray its unique position among the museums of the world.

These collections include a world-famous assemblage of Chinese porcelains, mostly booty from the victorious Ottoman campaigns in Iran, Syria and Egypt in the earlier decades of the sixteenth century but subsequently augmented by gifts from tributaries and allies. This is exhibited in the palace kitchens, which owe their distinctive appearance to restorations following a serious fire in 1574. There is also an important collection of clocks and watches, remaining from the European gifts of time-pieces and mechanical instruments for which the Sultans had such a passion that they even demanded them as tribute. The Armoury included splendid examples of arms and armour made for, or even, by the Ottoman Sultans, together with prize pieces from Alexandria (captured in 1517) and Mongol,

Turcoman and Safavid swords from victories at Başkent (1473) and Çaldıran (1514), as well as European arms and cannonry. The richest spoils are, however, now in the Treasury (Hazine) – jewels, jewellery, hardstones and goldsmith's work; and Korans, calligraphy and illustrated manuscripts and albums from Egypt, Syria, Mesopotamia, Iran, Central Asia and India: they are a tribute to the taste and discrimination of the conquering Ottoman rulers. Once in the palace, moreover, they were not hoarded avariciously but inspired Ottoman craftsmen to emulate them. The finest creations of sixteenth- and seventeenth-century Ottoman art, as the collection of Royal textiles and their designs bears witness, owe much of their individuality to such prototypes imitated or skilfully adapted to traditional Turkish taste.

An essential background to these splendid collections was provided by the textiles made for (or later probably in) the Palace, both jewelled gold embroideries for furnishing or luxurious floor-coverings, and brilliant silks made up either as garments for the Sultans and the princes or as robes of honour distributed to Ottoman officials or distinguished foreign visitors. Initially these were as much imports from Iran or Italy as products of the centre of the Turkish luxury textile industry, Bursa, where the Court, though evidently not controlling their manufacture in detail, was the principal customer. Later in the sixteenth century, looms were set up in Istanbul, where the craftsmen were in this case primarily responsible for fulfilling Court orders.

These Bursa and Istanbul silks are richly represented in cathedral treasuries and palace collections in Sweden, Russia and Eastern Europe, though even so they give little idea of the diversity and sheer volume of production of the Ottoman looms. In the Topkapı Saray, on the other hand, it was customary for the wardrobes of Sultans, members of the Royal family, and even viziers on their death or disgrace to be registered and stored in the palace. These were periodically inspected but although as a result the labels on some of them have been lost or misplaced, the collection which was revealed following the Turkish revolution of 1924 was dazzling in its abundance and variety. It is this collection, augmented by robes and embroideries from the Royal mausolea, where they were customarily draped over cenotaphs, which forms the subject of the present volume.

PART I
Costumes

1

The collections of Sultans' and other Ottoman costumes and embroideries in the Topkapı Saray and their history

As early as the mid-nineteenth century some of the historic Imperial costumes from the Topkapı Saray collections were put on display in the Treasury[1] though, as A. J. B. Wace, who saw them in 1903, noted, special permission had to be obtained to see them.[2] With the transformation of the Topkapı Saray into a museum after the Revolution, the costumes were taken out of storage, repaired and in 1964 were placed on permanent exhibition in the Topkapı Saray, in the Seferli Koğuşu (the 'Campaign Dormitory'),[3] appropriately, for under the Ottomans the duties of its employees included the care of the Sultan's wardrobe. It was instituted by Murād IV in 1046/1636–7, just before he set out on his Transcaucasian campaign.

The collections contain almost 2,500 pieces. Of these some six hundred selected items are at present exhibited in chronological sequence, though few of the enormous number of Imperial undergarments are displayed. They are virtually all men's clothing: the clothes of the ladies of the Court and the Harem have nearly all vanished without trace, though it has been possible to add three or four pieces by purchase since the creation of the Topkapı Saray Museum. The rich collection of men's clothes is in fact the result of a happy accident, arising from the custom (apparently not peculiar to the Ottomans) that, on the death of a Sultan, a prince (Şehzāde) and sometimes even a vizier,[4] the belongings of the deceased, including his clothes, were not sold or distributed among his heirs but were bundled up in wrappers (*bohça*) and registered in the Treasury. This practice has more than anything contributed to their preservation though not, unfortunately, to their correct identification. Lists of these belongings certainly exist, but practically all contain evident inaccuracies. This is because at various intervals the bundles were unwrapped for inspection, and when they were wrapped up again some of the labels must have got mixed up. Moreover, such was the Ottoman Sultans' pride in their lineage that they were too ready to attribute garments labelled 'Murād' or 'Meḥmed' or 'ʿOsmān' to the first ruler of that name. These speculative and often frankly unconvincing attributions were recorded and were then uncritically repeated in later registers.[5]

Extracts from the register made for Muṣṭafā III in 1760 have been published by Tahsin Öz, as follows:[6]

*Kiswa*s of the Sultans of past ages: of Sultan Muṣṭafā Ḫān, 1 wrapper; of Sultan ʿOsmān Ġāzī [i.e. the founder of the dynasty, 1281–*c.*1324], 3 wrappers; the gold crown(?) [*tāc*] of Sulṭān Meḥmed, son of Yıldırım Bāyazīd [Meḥmed I, 1403]; *kiswa*s of Meḥmed II Fātiḥ, of Selīm I and of Şehzāde Meḥmed, son of Süleymān the Magnificent, 2 wrappers; *kiswa*s of Selīm I, originally 3 wrappers, now 2; *kiswa*s of Süleymān the Magnificent, 12 wrappers; *kiswa*s of Süleymān and Selīm [II, 1566–74], 1 wrapper; *kiswa*s of Süleymān, Selīm, Murād [III, 1574–95] and Meḥmed [III, 1595–1603], 1 wrapper; *kiswa*s of Murād III, 1 wrapper; *kiswa*s of Murād Ḫān [Murād II(?), 1421–51] and Meḥmed [II(?), 1451–81], 1 wrapper; *kiswa*s of Meḥmed Ḫān Ġāzī (? II), a wrapper and an oil-cloth; *kiswa*s of Aḥmed Ḫān, who built the mosque [Aḥmed I, 1603–17], 2 wrappers; the spare skull-caps (*ʿimāme*) of the latter, 1 wrapper; *kiswa*s of the murdered ʿOsmān [II, 1618–22], 3 wrappers; *kiswa*s of Murād, conqueror of Baghdad [Murād IV, 1623–40], 6 wrappers and oil-cloths; *kiswa*s of Aḥmed III [1703–30], 1 wrapper; spare *kiswa*s belonging to the latter, 1 wrapper; *kiswa*s of Maḥmūd Ḫān [I, 1730–54], 1 wrapper; *kiswa*s of unknown rulers of the past, 12 wrappers; *kiswa*s of Murād Ḫān [? Murād II], 2 wrappers; turbans and skull-caps of the latter, 1 wrapper; headgear of various types of an unknown ruler; dyed animal skins, 1 wrapper; red felt banner bags and other cloths of past rulers, 1 wrapper; *kiswa*s of Sultan Selīm [?], 1 wrapper; *kiswa*s of Sultan Muṣṭafā [? Muṣṭafā II, 1695–1703], 1 wrapper; clothes worn by Sultan Murād [?] as a prince 1 small wrapper; clothes worn by Sultan Aḥmed as a prince [? Aḥmed I, 1603–17], 1 small wrapper; specimen clothes of princes and Sultans, 1 large oil-cloth; specimen princes' clothes, 1 wrapper; short tunics or jackets [*nīmten, mintāne*] of cloth of gold, of Sultan Murād and Sultan Meḥmed [?], 1 wrapper; satin-covered chain-mail of Aḥmed, the founder of the mosque [I, 1603–17], 1 wrapper; *kiswas* of 'Sultan Ḳāsim', 1 wrapper; specimen *kiswa* and rainwear [*yağmurluk*] from the Hırka-i Saadet Dairesi [Pavilion of the Mantle of the Prophet], 1 oil-cloth; *kiswas* borne in procession by rulers of the past from Baghdad to Diyarbekir, 1 oil-cloth; swaddling clothes of rulers of the past, 1 oil-cloth; blankets etc., 1 oil-cloth.

At first sight this list exemplifies the maddening tendency of Ottoman registers to specify in detail items quite different from what they are in reality. Since *kiswas* were not 'garments' but were specially made for presentation to the Kaʿba, why were there so many still in Muṣṭafā's Treasury? But, whether or not the attributions are correct, there is – as the dates I have added in square brackets show – quite a lot of internal evidence to identify the particular rulers, even if this cannot always be done, and it is evidently on the basis of this register that the clothes associated with Sultan Aḥmed I as a boy (*ills. 32–4*), for example, have been attributed in the present volume. But the considerable number of unattributed items in the Muṣṭafā III register also casts doubt on the actual attributions of cloths or clothing to the first Sultan so named.

Not all the labels are those stitched on in the later eighteenth century: some are earlier, and some later, and all or most may reflect a living tradition regarding the Sultan to whom the items supposedly belonged. Sometimes it is relatively easy to guess that the name is right but the actual identification wrong, as for example with the kaftan associated with 'Bāyazīd' (*ill. 18*), which cannot refer to Bāyazīd II (1481–1512), for the garment is datable stylistically to *c.* 1560, and thus could well have belonged to Şehzāde Bāyazīd, a prince who rebelled, deserted to the Safavids and was ultimately returned to Istanbul, where he was strangled in 1561. In other cases, however, the labels are uninformative, or suggest a wildly inappropriate attribution, e.g. a printed taffeta gown (*ill. 26*) which, though labelled as having belonged to Murād III (1574–95), is evidently a woman's garment. This explains, perhaps, some of the wide differences in dating and attribution which have been given to certain silks in the Topkapı Saray collection.

To attempt to attribute all the kaftans in the Topkapı Saray collections on the basis of such eccentric inventories would be a hopeless task. There is, however, a fortunate circumstance which also preserved kaftans of identifiable Sultans and princes, namely that the corpses of deceased rulers and their sons were often wrapped in their kaftans, which might be used also to cover the bier. They were also spread over the cenotaphs in Royal tombs, and a substantial number of the princes' garments now in the Topkapı Saray collection were brought into the Palace in the late nineteenth century when the Royal tombs in Istanbul were cleared of their accumulated furniture, woodwork, glass, pottery mosque lamps and fine carpets. Not all were acquired, and it is to be presumed that those that were unwanted were sold on the market: these are principally in the Victoria and Albert Museum, London, and the Royal Scottish Museum in Edinburgh.

Mausoleums as such have not everywhere been approved of in Islam. The custom of furnishing them with rich coverings, carpets and decorative objects was even less acceptable. In the case of Ottoman Istanbul the practice may easily be ascribed to ancient Turkish customs, for Ibn Baṭṭūṭa, who travelled through Anatolia in the early 1330s, records similar customs in the principality of Saruhan.[7] When he arrived at the principal town, Maghnīsiyya (modern Manisa), he found the Sultan at the mausoleum of his son who had died some months before. The body had been embalmed and placed in a bier of wood with a lid of tinned iron: this was raised on high trestles in a domed chamber with a vent. Subsequently, he was told, the vault of the dome would be filled in and the boy's cenotaph placed where it could be seen at ground level, with his garments laid over it.

Ibn Baṭṭūṭa goes on to state that he had seen such practices observed by other rulers. None can have been more conspicuous than Tamerlane (Tīmūr), whose tomb at Samarkand, the Gūr-i Mīr, in a building originally intended to lodge only the remains of his grandson, Muḥammad Sulṭān, was bestrewn with his weapons, his personal possessions, and his clothes – at least until they were removed in 1409 by his son, Shāh Rukh, who found them irreligious.[8] The custom was evidently widespread, and those practising it included the Turkish rulers of Mamlūk Egypt, but the motivation and the symbolism of such grand funerary exhibits in their tradition remain to be explained. As for the Ottoman material, both in Istanbul and in European collections, the evidence from the Royal tombs in Istanbul has been regrettably weakened by the failure to record in appropriate detail the provenance of the surviving garments. Nevertheless, the stylistic evidence for dating, i.e. the kaftans attributable in periodic registers of the Imperial Treasury or Wardrobe and the tomb finds, tends to argue, cumulatively, for a chronology which, *faute de mieux*, is adopted in the present volume.

Textiles are diverse. As a result many significant types in the Topkapı Saray must be ignored. Among the garments not treated or illustrated in the present volume the most interesting are probably a series of 'talismanic shirts' (*yazılı gömlek*), conserved both in the Topkapı Saray collections and, scattered, in European collections too.[9] They are voluminous vests, half-length (*nīmten*, or *mintāne*), of fine linen or cotton (*bez*), printed or painted with Koranic inscriptions, prayers, mottoes, magic squares of varying degrees of complication and devices derived from contemporary manuscript illumination, in black, red, gold, green and dark blue. One of them in the Topkapı Saray[10] dated 14 Zilḥicce 881–16 Muḥarram 885/30 March 1477–29 March 1480 is in the name of Bāyazīd II's younger brother, the unfortunate Prince Cem, who spent most of his life in exile in the courts of Europe: it was never worn, for the opening for the head was never cut, but the decoration is so fine and elaborate that it could easily have taken longer to execute than the three years recorded in the inscription. These garments were almost certainly not underwear, since they were voluminous enough to go over a kaftan or a coat of mail, and the inscriptions they bear suggest that they were indeed talismanic, to protect the wearer in illness or in battle. It has, however, also been suggested that these were ceremonial garments, associated with the investiture of the prince or Sultan in one or other of the Ṣūfī orders which, out of policy as much as piety, they periodically patronized.

Other decorated textiles, cottons and linens, which figure prominently in, for example, the Treasury inventory of Bāyazīd II dated 910/1505, have not survived, nor has anything been identified which might give an idea of their appearance.[11] Of prime importance also were the Imperial tents, pitched both on campaigns and in the palace, pavilions, awnings and enclosures. The tents were of heavy cotton or hessian with elaborate decoration in appliqué cloth, but also with gold braiding and embroidery, and – with their own cushions, mattresses and kilims – made what was practically a portable palace. They are faithfully recorded in the illustrated Ottoman annals of the later sixteenth century, but they principally came to European notice with the booty taken after John Sobieski's relief of Vienna in 1683 and in the subsequent defeats of the Ottoman armies at Slankamen and Belgrade. The tents captured there are preserved in Kraków (the Wawel), Vienna (the Hofburg), Bavaria (Bayerisches Armeemuseum, Ingolstadt) and in other European museums, but the Topkapı Saray palace collection was, evidently for administrative reasons, installed in the Military Museum (Askeri Müze) at Harbiye in Istanbul.[12]

The vast size of these tents and their often poor state of preservation – for they were brought out, along with the weapons from the Armoury, time and time again whenever a campaign was to be equipped – make them difficult to display, but they were an essential feature of Ottoman military ceremonial. Some, moreover, were trophies. The Cairene historian, Ibn Iyās,[13] describes that brought by the Turcoman prince ʿAlī Dawlat as a gift to the Mamlūk Sultan al-Ghawrī in 1512. It was, he says, of multicoloured silk, its walls decorated with flowering trees full of birds: part of it was a wooden pavilion, painted pink and deep blue, with animals in combat and upholstered in blue woollen cloth, with braid and red silk pompons. This was very probably the tent which Tomà Mocenigo, who witnessed the celebrations attending the circumcision of Süleymān the Magnificent's sons, described in 1530.[14] Among the tents erected in the Hippodrome as trophies was that of the Mamlūk Sultan al-Ghawrī. Another tent described by Ibn Iyās had been made for the Sultan Qā'it Bāy (died 1496) at a cost of 36,000 dinars. This was of multicoloured appliqué cloth, with lofty reception halls and a domed central area pierced with windows of coloured glass: it took three hundred sailors to erect it. On al-Ghawrī's death, however, it was sold to Maghribī merchants and cut up into small pieces.

The importance of tents and tent-work might suggest that the Ottomans would appreciate European tapestries. Europeans certainly thought so. The Venetian ambassador, Trevisan, when in Cairo in 1512[15] hung the rooms of the palace where he was lodged with his own tapestries which he remarked were a novelty in Egypt but *'molto apreziate da more'*. In 1553 the Flemish tapestry designer, Peter Coecke van Aelst, published a series of prints after cartoons of Turkish subjects, including a funeral, which he had sketched while in Istanbul. These he evidently hoped to persuade the Ottoman Court to commission. His hopes were dashed, however. Indeed, a tapestry (showing the Emperor Charles V with the Imperial Habsburg regalia and the Electors and the notables of the Holy Roman Empire doing homage), which the French gem-merchant Jean Baptiste Tavernier saw in the early 1670s on a stand in one of the rooms of the Treasury in the Topkapı Saray,[16] had evidently never been brought out since its arrival as a diplomatic gift. Despite the comfort of Arras against the bitter winter winds from the Bosphorus, such gifts seem not to have been appreciated, partly because of the unsuitability of the subjects depicted, but also because there were in the Topkapı Saray practically no rooms of the right dimensions in which to hang them.

Finally, one must mention the inscribed woven silks in the Topkapı Saray, notably, *kiswa*s, tomb-covers and banners. The annual presentation of a veil (*kiswa*) for the Kaʿba was a jealously guarded prerogative, first of the ʿAbbāsid Caliphs in Baghdad, and one which, on the extinction of the Caliphate in 1258, passed to the

Mamlūk rulers of Egypt. They guarded this right equally jealously, for it symbolized their protectorate, as remunerative as it was prestigious, of the Holy Places of Islam.[17] With the Ottoman conquest of Egypt and of the Hijaz in 1516–17 the prerogative passed to Selīm I and his successors, though the *kiswa* long continued to be woven in Cairo: it was of plain black silk. Somewhat similar in conception were tomb-covers ordered for shrines and sometimes for rulers' tombs, normally with chevron bands of repeating Koranic or Royal inscriptions in white on red, green or black.

Banners, which are known from Italian booty, particularly Venetian (now in the Museo Correr, Venice), and from spoils of the Knights of Malta from Lepanto (1571), Alexandria (1602) and Bizerta (1675; fragments hung in the church of S. Stefano in Pisa), were mostly of heavy plain green or red silk, with bands or medallions of Koranic script, and often bore the two-pronged sword of ʿAlī, Dhu'l-Faqār, part of the legendary booty from the Battle of Badr in AD 624 and a striking symbol of victorious Islam. The mint condition of many of the Ottoman banners captured at the Relief of Vienna in 1683[18] suggests that such symbolic banners were often specially woven for a particular campaign and issued when the Paşa was commissioned to command it. Rather surprisingly, some examples bear nineteenth-century dates, indicating that they were copied under Selīm III or Maḥmūd II; these may have been commemorative, though the dates they bear do not appear to be particularly significant.

All these inscribed textiles must have been woven after cartoons, though like the banners they could have been easily mass-produced or re-woven to order, as required. They show up, however, one remarkable absence in the design of Bursa silk brocades, namely patterns with inscriptions. This is all the more interesting in that the tradition of presenting robes of honour which the Ottomans inherited was from its origins heavily dependent upon the Caliph or his representative, for by accepting the robe the receiver both put himself under his protection and also recognized his authority: garments bearing such *ṭirāz* inscriptions (i.e. the honorific titles of the Royal donor) were thus something in the way of a badge of service. This feature was equally central to the Mamlūk system of robes of honour (cf. Chapter 7). They were not just rewards for service but, as it were, part of the uniform allowance. One would naturally expect the Ottomans, with their strong adherence to Islamic tradition, to have taken this over as well. But, whereas figural Bursa silks are rare, Bursa silk fabrics bearing the name of an Ottoman Sultan are quite unknown. This represents a striking demonstration of the prevalence of taste over practical and symbolic utility.

Notes to Chapter 1

1 G. Noguès, 'Elbicéi Atika. Musée de costumes ottomanes à Constantinople', *Revue Orientale et Africaine* II (1852), 418–29.
2 Tahsin Öz, *Turkish Textiles and Velvets* (Ankara 1950), vi.
3 Ismail Hakkı Uzunçarşılı, 'Osmanlılar zamanında saraylarda musiki hayatı', *Belleten* XLI (1977), 87.
4 There is in the Topkapı Saray Archives an inventory (D.2787), datable post 978/1570–1, of some of the valuables which were surrendered to the Treasury on the death of Kara ʿOsmān Şāh Beg, whose grandmother was a daughter of Selīm I. The list is obviously not all his belongings, but may consist of objects, and one crimson velvet cloak (ʿ*abā*), which were personal gifts to him from the Sultan. Cf. I. H. Uzunçarşılı, 'Yavuz Sultan Selim'in kızı Hanım Sultan ve torunu Kara Osman Şah Bey vakfiyeleri', *Belleten* XL (1976), 467–78.
5 For example in an unpublished Palace inventory of 1091/1680–1 (Topkapı Saray Archives, D.12a–b).
6 Topkapı Saray Archives, D.2175. The translation given here is a précis from Tahsin Öz, *Türk Kumaş ve Kadifeleri* I (Istanbul 1946), 8–10. In the English edition (*Turkish Textiles and Velvets*, pp. 16–17), the term *kiswa*s – meaning, technically, veils ordered and presented by the Ottoman Sultans annually to the Kaʿba at Mecca, – is rendered simply as 'garments'. Cf. note 17, below.
7 *The Travels of Ibn Baṭṭūṭa, A.D. 1325–1354*, translated, with revisions and notes from the Arabic text edited by C. Defrémery and B. R. Sanguinetti, by H. A. R. Gibb, vol. II (Cambridge 1962), 447.
8 'V. V. Bartol'd's article "O pogrebenii Timura", translated by J. M. Rogers', *Iran* XII (1974), 65–87.
9 de Hammer [J. von Hammer-Purgstall], 'Observations sur les chemises talismaniques des musulmans et particulièrement sur celle qui se conserve dans le couvent des Cisterciens nommé Neukloster, près de Vienne en Autriche', *Journal Asiatique* IX (1832), 219–48. The same author published a second such shirt (then in the Arsenal in Vienna), in which Ḳara Muṣṭafā Paşa was buried at Belgrade *c.*1687; see *Wien's erste aufgehobene türkische Belagerung* (Vienna 1829), 122–36.
10 *The Anatolian Civilisations*, exhibition catalogue (Istanbul 1983), E 25.
11 Cf. J. M. Rogers, 'An Ottoman palace inventory of the reign of Bayazid II', *VIe Colloque du CIEPO, Cambridge 1984*, ed. J.-L. Bacqué-Grammont (Istanbul 1986); The inventory is dated 10 Şaʿbān 910/17 January 1505. It is, however, highly likely that the fine cottons were Indian and that many of them were block-printed. Cf. Mattiebelle Gissinger, *Master Dyers to the World. Technique and trade in early Indian dyed cotton textiles* (The Textile Museum, Washington, DC 1982).
12 The Topkapı Saray Museum has never had space to display the tents in its collection.
13 Gaston Wiet, *Journal d'un bourgeois du Caire* (Paris 1960) I, 234; ibid., II, 23, 167; also Gaston Wiet, *Histoire des Mamlouks circassiens* (Cairo 1945) II, 222, 241.
14 Marino Sanuto, *Diarii* LIII (Venice 1899), 443–58.
15 Ch. Schéfer (ed.), *Le voyage d'Outremer . . . de Jehan Thenaud, suivi de la relation de l'ambassade de Domenico Trevisan auprès du Soudan d'Egypte (1512)* (Paris 1874), 182–9.
16 *Nouvelle relation du Serrail du Grand Seigneur* (Paris 1675), 142.
17 *Encyclopaedia of Islam* (2nd ed.): entry 'Kiswa'; G. Wiet, 'L'Egypte et les lieux saints de l'Islam' in *Mélanges René Crozet* (Poitiers 1966), 119–30.
18 Zdzisław Żygulski, Jr, 'Chorągwie tureckie w Polsce', *Studia do Dziejów Wawelu* III (Kraków 1968), 363–433.

2

Silk textiles: geography and types

The concentration of the Ottoman silk industry upon Bursa (see Chapter 4) was partly for fiscal convenience (since it was immensely remunerative to the State at all stages of manufacture) and partly a consequence of that city's role as an entrepot in the international trade in raw silk. This was largely imported from Shīrvān in Azerbaijan and from Gīlān and Mazāndarān in Northern Iran and re-exported towards Europe. With the Ottoman-Safavid hostilities of the sixteenth century, this trade to Europe was constantly in danger of interruption, yet no satisfactory alternative entrepot developed, and the trade remained important enough for the Safavid Shah ʿAbbās I (1588–1629) to consider diverting it to Europe by the sea route, using English, Dutch or Portuguese carriers, and thus inflict a crushing blow on the Ottoman economy.[1] Iran also produced fine woven silks, and Yazd brocades (*kemḫā*) are frequently mentioned in Ottoman registers of the early sixteenth century, but their appearance is conjectural for there are practically no identifiable Persian silks dating from before 1600.

Velvets and brocades were also woven at provincial centres in the Ottoman Empire, *inter alia*, at Aleppo, Amasya, Kaffa (modern Feodosiya) in the Crimea, Mardin and on Chios. And, later in the sixteenth century, the Istanbul looms with weavers employed by the Palace, as well as looms manufacturing for the open market, come to the fore. It is, however, practically impossible to differentiate any of these fabrics, in quality, technique or pattern, even those made in Istanbul. And although, as in the 1640 Istanbul price register,[2] Bursa silks remained pre-eminent, there must have been many local imitations, doubtless of poorer quality. In the present state of our knowledge discussion of provenance is unhelpful, and in this volume 'Bursa' will be taken as a trade term, for silks of certain general descriptions, wherever they may actually have been made.

The technical identification and description of woven silks is also a matter of some complexity. Too little has been recorded of the types of looms employed by the Bursa weavers to disentangle the copious Ottoman terminology for silks, to match the terms with the equally rich Venetian and Genoese vocabulary or to propose, except in very few cases, English equivalents in technical terms. The following remarks relate, therefore, primarily to the Ottoman terms to be found in Palace inventories, registers and edicts, and with respect to the fabrics of the robes chosen here for illustration. It should, of course, be borne in mind that while both the Ottoman authorities and Italian merchants, customs officials and courtiers knew their fabrics and for the most part employ their terms consistently, the terminology for brocades, in particular suggests that they were not concerned to make the kind of distinctions which would interest us nowadays.

The fabrics illustrated here are mostly heavy silks – satins, velvets, brocades, brocaded velvets and cloth of gold or silver. Lighter fabrics were also made, like taffeta (*tafta*) and shot silk (*cānfes*: the term is used in modern Turkish as an equivalent for *tafta*). The inventories, moreover, list many fabrics for which it is difficult to find an identification.

Serāser (*ills. 9, 20, 32, 48, 50, 54, 58, 61, 64, 76, 79*) was used for cloths of gold or silver, that is lamé, in which the whole surface of the fabric was covered with metal thread, the pattern, if any, being generally indicated in outline in coloured silks. Pure gold was actually too soft for use as thread, so it was generally alloyed with silver. Alternatively, the silver thread was wrapped over a core of bright yellow silk, which gave a fair approximation to the appearance of real gold. The resultant fabrics were showy, heavy and immensely costly: they were primarily ordered for Sultans or the highest viziers, and the expense led to their manufacture in Istanbul, close to supervision from the Palace. The drain to the Mint in precious metals was such that the manufacture of such costly fabrics was constantly restricted, though even when the authorities did not forbid the manufacture of silver thread, particularly in the seventeenth century and later, the silver was increasingly debased with copper. Of some importance is a decree, dated 12 Ṣafar 985/1 May 1577,[3] ordering the number of *serāser* looms in Istanbul to be restricted to one hundred, 'as it was in the reigns of Süleymān the Magnificent and his father Selīm I'. The remaining looms were to be closed down, but, in order to avoid undue distress to the weavers, they would be permitted to weave *serenk* – silk brocaded satin – instead (see below).

These edicts cannot have been very effective for long, for they are regularly repeated in the seventeenth century. Moreover, *serāser* manufactured in Istanbul was sold on the open market in the mid-seventeenth century. The 1640 Istanbul price register (the tone of which is not sumptuary) categorizes different sorts of *serāser*,[4] prescribing the relative quantities of metal thread (*ṣırma*) on white or yellow silk cores, Bursa silk and silk from Persia or Tripoli in the Lebanon by weight for a fabric of standard length and weight. It also lists patterns – plane leaves, pomegranates, crescents, peacock's tail, flowers and checked designs (*ṣaṭranc*). The documents show that there were evidently different qualities of *serāser* available, though from the prices given in the 1640 register it is unclear whether that sold on the Istanbul market was identical or inferior to that furnished to the Court or to the Sultans' ministers.

Brocades (*çātma* and *kemḫā*, sometimes confusingly linked as *kemḫā-i çātma*) were of various types (*ills. 1, 14, 23, 27, 28, 31, 42, 43, 45–7, 49*).[5] Usage is not always consistent, but *çātma* in the present volume applies mainly to brocaded velvets (cf. *ill. 23*) in which gold or silver thread may play a conspicuous part: they were much used for cushion and bolster covers, as well as for sumptuous floor-coverings. *Çātma* continued to be woven in Istanbul until the eighteenth and nineteenth centuries, near the Ayazma Camii at Üsküdar (1170/1760–1), later looms being in the neighbourhood of the Selimiye Mosque, founded in 1204/1789–90 by Selīm III.

The term *kemḫā* seems to be applied more generally to brocades (*ills. 3, 7, 19, 29, 30, 33, 38, 44*), with or without silver or gold thread. In the *Diarii* of Marino Sanuto such fabrics seem to be termed indiscriminately *damaschin* or *brocha*. One of the most sumptuous of these is that possibly associated with Şehzāde Bāyazīd (strangled 1561), with a thread count of more than 8,000 as opposed to the stipulated count of 6,600 in the records of the Bursa kadi's court, and no repeat in the pattern (*ill. 18*). *Kemḫā* was much in demand from the Palace, and it is highly probable that much of this was woven in Istanbul on the Palace looms.[6] The officials who controlled its manufacture were correspondingly important. In 1650, for example, the Kemhacıbaşı (the head of the corporation of brocade weavers in Istanbul) was able to endow a mosque and its associated buildings, the Kemha Camii, near the Fethiye Camii (the former Byzantine church of the Pammakaristos) in Istanbul.

A simpler form of brocade was known as *serenk* or *kemḫā-i serenk* (literally, 3-coloured fabric). As the edict of 985/1577 suggests, it was evidently intended as a substitute for cloth of gold or silver, and the lavish use of bright yellow silk must have been to convey the effect of gold, but more cheaply (*ills. 6, 8*). Whether the patterns of these *serenk* fabrics were meant to reproduce those of cloth of gold is unclear. In fact, a large proportion of Bursa ogival or medallion silk brocades are three-colour – crimson, blue and yellow – and a considerable number of the *kemḫā* kaftans (*ills. 3, 7, 19, 29, 30, 33, 38, 44*) may thus be *serenk*.

Striped gold or silver brocades, many with minute repeating floral patterns under the strong influence of Lyons silks, were popular in the eighteenth century. These came to be known as *selīmiye*, from the looms established by Selīm III (1789–1807), near the Selimiye barracks in the neighbourhood of his mosque, Selimiye. Similar materials had earlier been made on the looms in the vicinity of the Ayazma Camii in Üsküdar (1170/1760–1), but even earlier is a '*selīmiye*' kaftan (*ill. 57*) made for Maḥmūd I (1730–54). At this time the material must have been sold under another name.

Velvets (*ḳadīfe*),[7] generally silk (*ills. 2, 11, 23, 24, 27, 55*), though cotton velvets are also known to have been made at Bursa, are listed in inventories and price registers as plain, or with metal thread (*telli*). Far fewer distinctions are made in the types of velvet woven, however, than in contemporary Italian craft manuals or silk-merchants' accounts,[8] which regularly mention cut velvets (presumably, with voided *ferronerie* designs); velvets with uncut pile (Ottoman, *riṣte*); and embossed or pile on pile velvets (*velluti alto e basso* or *veludi a due o tre peli*). These were familiar to officials in Ottoman Turkey in the early sixteenth century, for the gifts to the envoy of the Mamlūk Sultan al-Ghawrī (Cumādā I 909/November 1503)[9] included a robe of crimson pile on pile (*dū-hāvī*) Italian velvet with ermine trimmings and hemmed in gold. None may ever have been made in Ottoman Turkey, but Wulff's description of embossed velvets woven in Persia in more recent times may indicate that there was a similar industry in Turkey.[10]

Among the most popular silks for tailoring were satins (*aṭlas*; the Venetian equivalent seems to have been *raso*), which were also used for linings. The commonest colour was crimson (cf. *ill. 87*), sometimes with a fine stripe or with a fine chevron pattern (*ṭarāḳlı*), but moiré patterns in green, brown and black (*ills. 12, 13, 62, 73, 78*) were also much favoured. Satins were also in demand as a base for appliqué work, in cloth of gold or satin of a contrasting colour (*ills. 21, 51*), as well as for heavy embroideries, and were also enhanced with woven metal thread. In the 1640 Istanbul price register[11] the dearest satins listed are crimson, red and purple, patterned (*heftrenk*) satins being markedly cheaper. Istanbul satins are also much less expensive than their Florentine, Venetian or even, by this time, French equivalents, probably in part because of the transport costs. But even cheaper than the Istanbul satins were brocades and satins from Chios and silks from Aleppo and Damascus.

Notes to Chapter 2

1 R. W. Ferrier, 'The European diplomacy of Shāh ʿAbbās and the first Persian embassy to England', *Iran* XI (1975), 75–92. The plans were never realized.

2 M. S. Kütükoğlu, *Osmanlılarda narh müessesesi ve 1640 tarihli narh defteri* (Istanbul 1983), 113–22.

3 Ahmet Refik, *On altıncı asırda Istanbul hayatı (1553–1591)* (Istanbul 1935), 115, No. 24.

4 Kütükoğlu, op. cit., 117–22; cf. also M. Braun-Ronsdorf, 'Gold and silver fabrics from mediaeval to modern times', *CIBA Review* (1961–3), 2–16.

5 L. Mackie, 'Rugs and Textiles' in E. Atıl (ed.), *Turkish Art* (New York–Washington, DC 1981), 350 ff.

6 M. Braun-Ronsdorf, '"Silk damasks" and "linen damasks"', *CIBA Review* (1955), 3983–4002.

7 A. Latour, 'Velvet', *CIBA Review* No. 96 (February 1953), 3445–67.

8 F. Edler de Roover, 'Andrea Banchi, Florentine silk manufacturer and merchant in the fifteenth century', *Studies in Medieval and Renaissance History* III (Lincoln, Nebraska 1966), 223–85.

9 Ö. L. Barkan, 'Istanbul saraylarına ait muhasebe defterleri', *Belgeler* IX (1979), 181, Item 193(ii).

10 H. E. Wulff, *The traditional crafts of Persia* (MIT Press, Cambridge, Mass. 1966), 172 ff.

11 Kütükoğlu, op. cit., 113–17.

3

Dyes and dyestuffs

THE basic information on dyes and dyestuffs used in Ottoman Turkey derives from lists of colourants and dyed fabrics in Ottoman inventories and other documents; from the actual colours of the surviving fabrics, which may often clarify the sense of otherwise obscure colour-words; and from Muslim or Italian manuals of dyes and dyeing prepared by guild masters. These last[1] are particularly important for the indications they give of the effects intended or required and their distinctions between dyes for different animal or plant fibres and, for example, leather.

The standard mordant (the agent necessary for the full development of the colours and for the fixing of the dyes to the fibres) was alum. The much greater range of colours available to dyers in seventeenth-century Europe depended upon experiments with other mordants, notably chrome and tin. In contrast to Renaissance Italy, where woad was still widely used to give a range of blues, the main Ottoman source was indigo (*nīl, çivit*) from *Indigofera tinctoria*, which mostly came with the spices from India via Egypt or the Hijaz. It was also used with henna, double-dyed to give a strong and lustrous black, and was particularly in demand as a hair dye. The Italian dyers also used a lichen, archil (*oricello*), related to litmus. This, like turnsole (*Crozophora tinctoria*), is an indicator, and, depending upon the acid or the alkaline environment, gives a range of colours from pink to purplish blue. Indigo was also important in dyeing in crimson and, with lac, kermes or cochineal, could also give a range of deep purples.

The most common yellow dye was obtained from safflower (*Carthamus tinctorius*), which was grown in Egypt and Iran as a commercial crop and which gives colours ranging from orange to a vivid golden yellow. Equally fine, though much more expensive, was saffron, from Spain, which was mostly used for silks. There are mentions of other dyestuffs in the documents – turmeric, buckthorn (*Rhamnus infectorius*) and the dyer's oak (*Quercus infectoria* and *Q. lusitanica*). These were certainly used in cottage industries, for leather and for the dyeing of wool for carpets; but the only 'peasant' dye regularly recorded by naturalists as having been used for yellow for silk seems to have been the yellow larkspur (*Delphinium zalil*), which, with alum as a mordant, gives a fast yellow, and, when used with copper sulphate, a clear green. In Ottoman Turkish this dye is known as *isperek*.

Green dyes could be obtained from the berries of two other buckthorns (*Rhamnus chlorophorus* and *Rh. utilis*), and under the name 'Persian berries' they were much used in Europe in the seventeenth–eighteenth centuries to give a brilliant green. Greens, however, were mostly the product of double dyeing, for most of the yellow plant dyes went well over an indigo base.

Sub-fusc colours present more of a problem. The 1505 Treasury inventory of Bāyazīd II lists dark grey (*surmaī*), brown or beige (*ʿasalī*, literally, honey-coloured) and black (*siyāh*) materials, but these silks are all Italian. G. Roseto's *Plictho* gives several recipes for dyeing black, most of which involve the use of oak galls (*māzū*) and iron vitriol (ferrous sulphate). The several alternatives suggest that none was wholly satisfactory and indeed the resulting dye (which was also commonly used for inks) has a notorious tendency to rot organic fibres. Black for garments, according to Busbecq, whose Counter-Reformation sobriety in dress at times aroused the reproach of Ottoman officials while he was in Istanbul in the 1550s, was highly unpopular at the Ottoman Court, though Süleymān the Magnificent as an elderly man certainly wore dark grey. It might well be, however, that the sub-fusc silks listed in inventories were all imported from Italy.

By far the largest range of dyestuffs available in Ottoman Turkey, however, lay in the brown-red-purple part of the spectrum. Madder, which had been cultivated since ancient times in Turkey and Iran, was of immense importance in the dyeing of wool for carpets, where the bright red known as 'Turkey red' was particularly favoured. It was also exported to Europe. If, however, it was used for silk-dyeing, the sources ignore it. Other vegetable dyes in this colour range seem to have been used for the colour *ṭāvūsī* (a calque on

Northern Italian *paonazzo*, which, somewhat unexpectedly, was the term for ecclesiastical Lenten purple), but though the plant used is sometimes mentioned (*şukūfe-i gügeygīz*; cf. modern Turkish *güveyiz*, rose-pink), quite frequently its identity is not known. Brazil-wood (*çūb-i baḳḳām*; Venetian *verzino*), which was so called long before the discovery of America, was also imported in quantity from Ceylon and gave a deep purplish-red. The proper identification of these and other vegetable dyes is, however, impossible without scientific analysis.

By far the most important sources of red and crimson (which word derives from the Turkish *kırmızı*) was a series of aphids and scale insects, the dried bodies of which gave a rich, expensive, glowing colour to velvets and satins and which, as *grana*, made the reputation of the Northern Italian silk-dyers. The most widespread of these was the kermes (*Kermococcus vermilio*, formerly *Coccus ilicis*), which infests the branches of the Kermes oak (*Quercus coccifera*), a species which grows all round the Mediterranean. The best dyes were held to come from Spain, Tunisia (Barbary) and Western Anatolia. An expensive crimson was also produced in Eastern Anatolia and Transcaucasia from an aphid, *Porphyrophora Hamelii*,[2] while a related species, *Porphyrophora polonica*, yielded 'St John's blood' or Polish cochineal, the least esteemed of all the crimson or scarlet dyestuffs. In Ottoman Turkey the favourite crimson seems to have been lac-crimson, imported in enormous quantities from India, where the lac insect infests species of *Ficus* and produces shellac.

A further development in crimson dyes resulted from the discovery of the Mexican scale insect, *Coccus cacti*, which produced the true cochineal, a brilliant, intense carmine. This had been introduced into Europe in 1520–30 and by 1560 had become the most esteemed of all the reds. By the early seventeenth century it had been found, moreover, that a chrome, rather than an alum, mordant produced the now familiar brilliant fiery scarlet. How far Mexican cochineal superseded lac and kermes in later Ottoman Turkey is so far obscure. However, it was very probably being imported in small quantities by the later sixteenth century, for suddenly carmine ink begins to be used for Imperial monograms (*tuğras*) on documents of State and for the most sumptuous illumination of Korans ordered by Murād III (1574–95). Carmine inks had, of course, been known before that, but had never been considered grand enough to use for such effects. Much progress has recently been made in the identification of carmine and crimson dyes from insect sources, and though molecular analysis may not solve all the problems, it may make it possible to show clearly patterns of change or taste in the exact tones of colour that were in favour at any particular time.

Notes to Chapter 3

1 In particular, Giovanventura Rosetti (Roseto), *The Plictho, Instructions in the Art of the Dyers, which teaches the dyeing of woolen Clothes, Linens, Cottons and Silk, by the Great Art as well as by the Common*, translation of the first edition of 1548, by S. M. Edelstein and H. C. Borghetty (Cambridge, Mass. 1969). Cf. also M. Levy, 'Medieval Arabic book binding and its relation to early chemistry and pharmacology', *Transactions of the American Philosophical Society*, NS 52/4 (1962), 1–79.

2 J. H. Hofenk-De Graaf, 'The chemistry of red dyestuffs in medieval and early modern Europe' in N. B. Harte and K. G. Ponting (eds.), *Cloth and clothing in medieval Europe. Essays in memory of Professor E. M. Carus-Wilson* (London 1983), 71–8; J. H. Munro, 'The medieval scarlet and the economics of sartorial splendour', ibid., 13–69.

4

The silk industry: organization

THE abundant evidence of edicts issued by the Ottoman central authorities, and of the records from the kadis' courts at Istanbul, Edirne, Ankara and Bursa has suggested to many recent historians of sixteenth- and seventeenth-century Ottoman Turkey that demand was pre-eminently stimulated by the Court, which had primacy of means and priority of choice. To supply it, they also assume, there were strictly controlled Court workshops (*kārhāne-i Ḫāṣṣa*), 'machineless factories' for the manufacture of luxuries and strategic materials. Outside the Court, supply and demand, of staple goods as well as luxuries, were regulated by comprehensive codes (*ḳānūnnāme-i iḥtisāb*) and registers fixing prices and profits (*narḫ*), as well as periodic sumptuary edicts, with a group of State merchants (*Ḫāṣṣa tuccārları*) to maintain control over the wholesale market and international trade.

This picture argues for a high, if periodically variable, degree of dirigisme in the Ottoman economy, both in production and consumption, though it is anachronistic to suppose that all these controls were present or exercised at all periods. The Court workshops, for example, are very much a phenomenon of the later sixteenth century, when their scope and number considerably increased. But although it involves oversimplification in every respect, it represents, probably, the Ottomans' own ideas of their economy, which would have satisfied even Colbert. However, by contrast with our knowledge of the Court factories established in France by Colbert under Louis XIV,[1] we have practically no idea of exactly why the Court factories in Istanbul were established or of their effect on supply and demand outside them. In fact the practice of the Ottoman authorities was much less dirigiste than their aims. In the silk industry, in particular, their interference seems to have been sporadic and unsystematic: for greater success, indeed, they should have interfered far more.[2]

The earliest relevant edict issued by the Ottoman central authorities is the 1502 Bursa *ḳānūnnāme-i iḥtisab* regulating prices and production for the market; dating from the reign of Bāyazīd II, it is – like other Ottoman edicts of this type, – far from comprehensive.[3] This is evidently because they were not systematic but were all *ad hoc* attempts to deal with abuses as they were brought to public notice: by customers, for example, against overcharging; by one trade against another, alleging unfair discrimination; or by the authorities, against the manufacturers. In the Bursa *ḳānūnnāme* they are directed against the silk manufacturers, spinners, dyers and weavers, and are couched in terms of an indictment, that since the reign of Meḥmed II of glorious memory all sorts of abuses had crept in and the quality had as a result much deteriorated. The dyers are accused specifically of reducing the amount of lac crimson and increasing the indigo, so that the colour was between crimson and violet; gold thread had been sophisticated by the spinners; and thread-counts, loom-widths and standard lengths had been steadily reduced by the weavers. Oddly, however, there are no accusations of sub-standard materials because of weaving faults: as if the weavers were assumed to be dishonest but competent. There follow thread-counts for gold velvets (*müzehheb ḳadīfe*), brocades, some of them flowered (*gulistānī kemḫā*), satins, taffetas, tabby weaves, crepe (*bürüncük*) and other fabrics, as well as precise specifications of the lengths of cloth tailors are to use for kaftans – sleeves, collar, skirt and body, and the number of pelts furriers are to incorporate into linings. These latter specifications are significant, if odd, for they suggest that such lined kaftans were not meant to fit anyone in particular but were thought of as being a single standard size.

If standards and quality had been continuously controlled, such abuses should never have crept in. But anyway even experts can hardly have been competent to pronounce confidently in 1502 on standards in the reign of Meḥmed II, who died in 1481. Why, moreover, should it have been the silk industry which was singled out for regulation? The answer is suggested by the records of honoraria and gratuities (*en'ām defterleri*) which have survived for the year 909/1503–4[4] and which list the seasonal allowances at the Court of Bāyazīd II to the Sultan's family, visiting ambassadors, viziers, and miscellaneous officials, craftsmen, huntsmen and spies. When not in cash, the allowances or rewards are practically all stipulated in silks or garments (even for the Court tailor), and though the list may not be exhaustive the consumption was undoubtedly vast. Textiles were thus the currency of the Ottoman honours system: for this to function properly it was essential both that the Palace should have full value for money and that the traditional standards should be maintained. This explains the tone of the allegations in the 1502 Bursa *ḳānūnnāme* against the spinners, dyers and weavers as if they were delinquent Court employees (which they were almost certainly not): simply, their silks played an essential official role. It also explains the specifications to tailors without provision for the size, age or sex of the customer, an unreasonable limitation of their practical utility had the tailors at Bursa been making garments for the retail market, but much less important if the robes were honorific.

Public honours systems notoriously fail to please. In Ottoman Turkey many of those who received robes of honour must have been far happier with cash, so that following the presentation there was no doubt a good deal of surreptitious trading-in at the Imperial Wardrobe. The estate of Süleymān Ağa, late Bostancıbaşı ('Chief Gardener') at the palace at Edirne[5] (1 Muḥarram 1014/19 May 1605), which included a wardrobe of satin, moiré and brocade robes, with sable, wolf and lynx fur trimmings, valued at 12,000 akçe each (three times his dearest male slaves and twice his most expensive concubines), is certainly evidence that high Court officials might keep some of the expensive robes presented to them. But, inescapably, such silks were so expensive to produce that without substantial recycling the cash drain on the Imperial treasury would have been intolerable.

An equally important reason for the regulation of the silk industry in the 1502 Bursa *ḳānūnnāme* was its social and economic structure, which was apparently so inefficient that constant regulations should have been required, instead of this single edict, to keep it functioning properly. It was indeed regulated by guilds, whose officials had some say as expert advisers (*ehl-i ḫibre*) in the fixing of prices and profits. They may even, by fixing terms of apprenticeship and by inspection of apprentices' work, have played some role in the control of quality. That was, however, by no means their principal function, which was essentially restrictive, to protect the members from competition from outsiders, and not to make weaving a more productive or efficient industry. Production was essentially domestic, with independent weavers employing indentured labour, mostly enslaved prisoners of war, on contract (*mukātebe*), who were to receive their freedom following the manufacture of a stipulated quantity of thread, cloth or garments. Many of the weavers were themselves freed slaves[6] whose own apprenticeship was doubtless served while they fulfilled the terms of the contract. They were left to find their own capital and even to finance the spinning of thread for the slaves, apprentices and journeymen weavers they employed at their looms. The silks they manufactured were then sold, at regulated prices, on the market in Bursa.

There is much to be learned from contemporary Italy of the way the silk-weaving industry must have worked in sixteenth-century Bursa. Silk industries demanded highly skilled craftsmen and were thus highly specialized, not just in the various stages of spinning and dyeing but also in the particular fabrics any weaver was capable of manufacturing; for each – pile velvets, satins, brocades or brocaded velvets – demanded different expertise and skills. Secondly, complex silks were highly labour intensive: in Florence in the fifteenth–sixteenth centuries, a loom-piece 40 *braccia* in length of *velluto alto basso brocato* (double- or triple-pile brocaded velvet) took a skilled craftsman six months to weave, and even much less technically complex fabrics might require a matter of weeks or even months.[7] Basic materials, moreover, were costly and the risk of pilferage high.[8] The lengthy manufacturing processes and high prime cost therefore made supervision essential at all stages of manufacture, all the more so in that, whereas mistakes in the processes preceding weaving could sometimes be corrected, silks, unlike woollens, underwent no finishing process, so that any weaving faults were practically impossible to gloss over.

In Italy in the fifteenth–sixteenth centuries, unlike Bursa where the constant, often exorbitant, Court demand absorbed everything the silk-weavers produced, the merchants who employed the weavers had to look for customers. Supervision of quality therefore devolved upon them and upon the guilds or corporations grouped into the *Arte della Seta* in various Italian cities, the statutes of which prescribed strict standards for membership and for the quality of fabrics, with severe, if sometimes obscure, sanctions against craftsmen who failed to observe them. However, a curious resemblance to the regulations in the 1502 Bursa *ḳānūnnāme* is to be found in the statutes of the Genoese *Arte della Seta*[9] which concentrate on thread-counts, weights and the right loom-lengths to the exclusion of quality, which, obviously, they should have put first. Even with stringent supervision, the Italian silk-weaving industries could not always have worked well.

But at Bursa the weaving guilds did not have the supervisory function of the *Arte delle Seta* and, apart from the 1502 *ḳānūnnāme*, there is practically no evidence of any attempt by the Court to impose standards through inspection, the Court officials appointed to oversee the industry having largely financial responsibilities. The concentration on the silk industry in the 1502 Bursa *ḳānūnnāme* is therefore comprehensible enough, but for Court interference to have been effective there should have been more of it and at all sorts of levels.

It has sometimes been assumed that the use of slaves under contract by the Bursa weavers was a contribution to the efficiency of the industry; but the very reverse must be the case. The slaves were a motley collection of prisoners of war – Bosnians, Russians, Greeks (*Rūm*), Italians (*Efrenc*), Vlachs, Circassians (*Çerkes*), Albanians, Hungarians and Croats, with a few Indians and Egyptians to confuse things – and their recruitment for a luxury textile industry must have been a desperate expedient in the face of an acute shortage of skilled labour. The most probable explanation of the financial aspects of the contracts is that the amounts represented a notional ransom which the slaves had to work off. The amounts, however, are not only rather small but also do not vary much: considering that the labour market must have shown periodic fluctuations and that, in the case of free individuals who bound themselves by contract, the price agreed must have varied with the weaver's need, the individual's need to tie his labour and his known or believed skill, the lack of variation is strange.

The prisoners of war may, of course, even if against all appearances, have been weavers by trade, for the Ottomans are known on occasion to have conscripted groups of craftsmen from Balkan or Hungarian towns and fortresses as they captured them. Alternatively, they may have been trained between their capture and the date the contracts were drawn up. In any case, their recruitment could well have been staggered so as to minimize the disruption a newcomer would inevitably cause to a workshop. But the system seems to have given too many hostages to fortune: what would happen if, for example, the *mukātebe* slave proved incapable of executing the contracted work to time? or what if he was simply incompetent? That an inefficient, even highly inefficient, system was adopted is, however, no evidence that the weavers were being foolish: they may simply have had no choice. Precious silks were essential to the Ottoman Court, both for its own needs and for the proper functioning of the Ottoman honours system. Demand was heavy, unpredictable, and invariably imperative: orders were to be fulfilled immediately. The weavers must therefore have turned to the *mukātebe* slaves, discounting obvious long-term disadvantages in efficiency, immediate productivity or even financial loss in favour of the rapid satisfaction of increasingly urgent demands. The fact that the system was plainly far from ideal either for the Bursa weavers or, ultimately, for the Ottoman authorities may, of course, explain why slaves under contract do not appear to have been employed in any other of the Ottoman luxury trades.

The results of these practices at Bursa in the late fifteenth and early sixteenth centuries doubtless explain why later in the sixteenth century the authorities increasingly turned to Court workshop looms (*kārḫāne-i ʿĀmire, kārḫāne-i Ḫāṣṣa*) as a solution to hiccoughs in production.[10] Since there is practically nothing surviving which can confidently be attributed to them, however, it is difficult to say either if they had an immediate effect on the quality of silks manufactured or if they then became responsible for catering for total demand from the Court, leaving the Bursa weavers to manufacture for the private market. The production of other salaried Ottoman Court workshops in the later sixteenth century (with the exception of the *nakkaşhane* or Court studio) would seem in practice to have been occasional rather than continuous; their employees also worked for the private sector; and appointment to them may have been partly honorific, as with the British list of Royal warrant-holders who supply goods and services at the present day. Undoubtedly, however, their ready accessibility, inside or near the palaces, gave the Court priority in the execution of commissions: presumably, only when these had been satisfactorily executed could they turn to private customers. This implies that, possibly in contrast to the Bursa weavers, they were anyway an élite.

The creation of the Court workshops seems to have been the result of a gradual process and, in the case of the silk weavers, one can identify a transitional period before their establishment in Istanbul. Associated with this is an interesting record of *c.*1530[11] of Hungarian, Bosnian, Italian, Circassian and other craftsmen apprenticed by name to master-weavers at Bursa, together with indications of the specific type of fabric each was to weave, whether brocaded velvets, medallion silks (?) (*benek*), multicoloured brocades (*heftrenk*), taffetas (*tafta*) or heavy floor-coverings (*döşeme*). Whether they were slaves or prisoners of war is not stated, but the order originated with Süleymān the Magnificent's favourite vizier, Ibrāhīm Paşa, which makes the requirements of apprenticeship and specialization particularly significant. Development in any case was rapid. By 1557 the Court looms employed 145 weavers and, although their numbers fluctuated a good deal in subsequent decades, a survey carried out in 1577 showed that, probably in addition to these Court employees, 88 of the 268 private looms operating in Istanbul were worked by slaves for the Palace.

Up to the establishment of the Court looms in Istanbul there is little if any evidence for systematic control of the silk-weaving industry by the Ottoman authorities. Nor, even subsequently, is there conclusive evidence that any silks were woven to designs provided by the Court. This must be emphasized for it is often held that the *nakkaşhane*, the Court studio responsible for producing books and albums for the Palace library, functioned as a sort of design centre, issuing patterns to other Court workshops in all sorts of media. In practice, this cannot have been the case; any such control would have amounted to dirigisme far beyond even that practised by Colbert in France in the seventeenth century. The *nakkaşhane* was certainly highly organized, but it must have been kept fully occupied with the writing, illustration, illumination and binding of the books and albums that the Sultans ordered.

Interestingly, documents on the silk industry scarcely ever refer to designers at all. In Genoa the only reference is a statute of the *Arte della Seta* prohibiting weavers from using each others' designs, though it is unclear why.[12] In Florence in the fifteenth–sixteenth centuries, the Banchi firm[13] used two designers, father and son, for cartoons for voided velvets (*zetani avellutati*) for brocaded pile on pile velvets (*velluti alto e basso in 3 alti di pelo*) and for brocaded polychrome damask. The Bursa documents tell us nothing. The Florentine father and son pair is, however, a significant indication that designing silks was also a specialized skill and as such was passed down in families. Though some Italian painters, notably Pisanello, Jacopo Bellini and Antonio Pollaiuolo, are credited with silk designs, it is improbable that an inexperienced designer could have produced a workable design. In particular, the use of heavy metal thread in brocades affected the fall as well as the overall weight of the fabric, and an inexpertly balanced design would result in a fabric which pulled away or sagged. The more complex the fabric (and Bursa silks are often no less complex than their Italian contemporaries), the more the designs required series of cartoons, and although part of the expertise of a master-weaver doubtless lay in his ability to set up his loom from a single cartoon for a pile velvet or a brocade, the provision of workable brocades demanded consultation between designer and weaver.

It follows that silk-designing was a skill beyond the capacity of a draughtsman not familiar with the mechanics of weaving, the behaviour of fabrics and the practical translation of sketches into workable patterns. The *nakkaşhane* could not have done this even if it had tried; nor is there anything remotely resembling a silk design in the Topkapı Saray Library. The presence of favourite Ottoman Court motifs of the later sixteenth century – cloud-bands, triple spots, florists' flowers – adapted or worked in to Bursa medallion silks is no argument either. The Bursa weavers were responsive enough to Court fashion, but practical considerations demanded their adaptation to suit their particular medium. By 1500 the Ottoman Empire was indeed a great bureaucracy. However, its treatment of the Bursa weavers gives no reason to believe that it was any more efficient or systematic than any other great bureaucracy the world has ever known. In particular, if what the authorities had wanted was an industry which gave them a monopoly of fine silks designed to their taste to fit in with designs for all sorts of luxury objects and materials, the weavers would have been controlled continuously and would have made different silks.

NOTES TO CHAPTER 4

1 Germain Martin, *La grande industrie sous le règne de Louis XIV (plus particulièrement de 1660 à 1715)* (Paris 1899), 7–18, 153–99.

2 The Bursa silk industry has been most effectively studied by Halil Inalcık; see bibliography in entry 'Ḥarīr', *Encyclopaedia of Islam* (2nd ed.), and an important addendum, 'Osmanlı idare, sosyal ve ekonomik tarihiyle ilgili belgeler: Bursa kadı sicillerinden seçmeler', *Belgeler* X (Ankara 1980–1), 1–91. Also important are F. Dalsar, *Türk sanayi ve ticaret tarihinde Bursa'da ipekçilik* (Istanbul 1960), and Halil Sahillioğlu, 'On beşinci yüzyıl sonunda Bursa iş ve sanayi hayatı kölelikten patronluğa', in *Mémorial Ömer Lûtfi Barkan* (Paris 1980), 179–88. Murat Çızakça's 'Price history and the Bursa silk industry: A study in Ottoman industrial decline 1550–1650' in *Journal of Economic History* 40 (1980), 533–50, and 'A short history of the Bursa silk industry (1500–1900)' in *Journal of the Economic and Social History of the Orient* 23 (1980), 142–52, are less concerned with the problems of internal structure than with the role of Bursa in the international trade in raw silk.

3 Ö. L. Barkan, 'XV asrın sonunda bazı büyük şehirlerde eşya ve

yiyecek fiyatlarının tesbit ve teftiş hususlarının tanzim eden kanunlar. II. Kanunname-i ihtisab-i Bursa', *Tarih Vesikaları* II/7 (1942), 15–40.

4 Ö. L. Barkan, 'Istanbul saraylarına ait muhasebe defterleri', *Belgeler* IX (Ankara 1979), 296–380.

5 Ö. L. Barkan, 'Edirne askerî kassam'ına ait tereke defterleri', *Belgeler* III (Ankara 1966), 224–7.

6 H. Sahillioğlu, op. cit. (see note 2 above); H. Inalcık, 'Osmanlı idare, sosyal ve ekonomik tarihiyle ilgili belgeler: Bursa kadı sicillerinden seçmeler', *Belgeler* X (Ankara 1980–1), 1–91.

7 Florence Edler de Roover, 'Andrea Banchi, Florentine silk manufacturer and merchant in the fifteenth century', *Studies in Medieval and Renaissance History* III (Lincoln, Nebraska 1966), 223–85; Rosalia Bonito Fanelli, 'I drappi d'oro: Economia e moda a Firenze nel Cinquecento' in *Le Arti del Principato Mediceo* (Florence 1980), 407–26.

8 To prevent abuses, weavers were not permitted to undertake work before completing previous commissions, and there were strict limits to the amount of thread a weaver was allowed to have in his possession at one time. Cf. Romolo Broglio d'Ajano, 'L'Industria della seta a Venezia' in C. M. Cipolla (ed.), *Storia dell'economia italiana* (Turin 1959), 209–62.

9 P. Massa, 'L'Arte genovese della Seta nella normativa del XVo al XVIo secolo', *Atti della Società Ligure di Storia Patria*, n.s. X (Genoa 1970), 5–307, especially 159–82 and note 28.

10 The earliest reference appears to be in the Bursa palace kitchen accounts for the year 947/1540–1 (Barkan, 'Muhasebe defterleri', 287–8), with payments for silk, dyestuffs and dyeing for a *kārḫāne-i ʿĀmire* in Istanbul, and for thread (both warp and weft), with indications to the dyers of the colours to be used for each. These instructions show that the materials were for a workshop of *weavers*.

11 F. Dalsar, *Türk sanayi ve ticaret tarihinde Bursa'da ipekçilik* (Istanbul 1960), 319, No. 245.

12 G. Morazzoni, *Le stoffe genovesi* (Genoa 1941), 97–127.

13 Florence Edler de Roover, art. cit.

5

Garments: Fashion, style and pattern

FROM the Sultan down to the Court pages (*içoğlans*), official dress was simple. The undergarments were a loose shirt (*iç gömlek*) variously of wool (*ill. 84*), cotton or compound silk-cotton cloth (the weaving of which was a cottage industry), and baggy trousers (*şalvar*) fastened at the waist with a sash and with draw-strings at the ankles. Sometimes soft leather boots were attached. The trousers were mostly concealed by the over-garments, but for sports could be worn with a short kaftan (*ḥırḳa; ill. 6*), and accordingly were of wool, or of satin, brocade or other rich cloths.

Over the shirt and trousers was the inner kaftan (*fustān, dōlma*[1]), a long-sleeved, collarless tunic or gown reaching to the feet, buttoned down the front and sometimes with braid or frogging on the chest, and tied with a sash, which also served as a pocket. For these mohair or silk, of a weight appropriate to the season, were favoured; occasionally they were of a patterned brocade. The *ʿulamāʾ* (theologians and Islamic lawyers), with their strong disapproval of show in dress, favoured woollen gowns of similar cut known as *cibbe*, though the highest legal dignitaries, like the viziers and the Commanders-in-Chief, did not scruple to wear splendid silks.

The illustrated Ottoman annals of the later sixteenth century show that the pages at official receptions wore the *dōlma* alone. Other Court officials, up to the Sultan himself, wore over-garments, kaftans of various sorts, of rich material, often patterned, appropriate to the season, which for the winter were often quilted (*ills. 8, 10, 52*), as well as fur-lined (*ill. 3*) and trimmed. Such were also the robes of honour with which officials were invested on their appointment or promotion or with which foreign ambassadors were honoured when they were received in audience. It is not entirely clear how far such robes of honour should be distinguished from the everyday wear of the Court officials, who generally wore short-sleeved kaftans in plain colours, and from the ceremonial kaftans worn by Sultans, which were cut much more fully (*ills. 21, 23, 25*) with sweeping skirts and long sleeves (*ḳolluḳ*), which were sometimes added, reaching to the floor, in sumptuous materials with lavish gold braid and jewelled buttons. They seem to have been the Sultans' prerogative but could be distributed to their favourites as a special mark of regard (cf. Chapter 7). Even more lavish were *ḳapānīçes* (the term is probably of Slav origin), long-sleeved kaftans, open at the front, slit at the sides or with high collars, with sumptuous linings and trimmings. The Topkapı Palace register for the year 1091/1680–1[2] lists a number of these, including one of cloth of gold with sable lining and with diamond buttons and frogging thickly encrusted with diamonds. Occasionally such garments may have been presented to viziers, or to, for example, the Tatar Khāns of the Crimea who were pensioners of the Ottoman Sultans.

The sheer weight of the fabrics must have made it very difficult for anyone wearing full ceremonial dress to move far or fast. Yet those who have travelled in Turkey will know the amazing capacity of Anatolian peasants even in the height of summer, to wear layer upon layer of clothing. In winter, anyway, the Ottomans needed outer garments or cloaks (*ferāce, ḳaba*) of wool, felt or leather. These were often quite plain, and were a suitable disguise for Ottoman ladies in the street, but an embroidered and appliqué leather riding coat of the late sixteenth century from Borostyánkö (Bernstein) in Hungary (Hungarian National Museum, Budapest, 69.80.C),[3] with a broad collar and tailored as a short-sleeved kaftan, shows that winter comfort and protection against the elements could be quite compatible with outward show. Such may have been the garments often listed in inventories as *ḳōnṭōş*, a term of Polish origin. One is also brought to realize, however, that even in summer Ottoman officials must often have worn as many layers of clothing as do Anatolian peasants. In the *Diarii* of Marino Sanuto (cf. p. 32), the Venetian emissaries who went to visit the commander of the Ottoman fleet at Preveza in 1533 describe him as follows:[4]

> The commander is a youngish man of about thirty-eight or less, with reddish moustaches and a hand-

> some appearance. He wore a turban of the finest cloth; he was seated cross-legged in the Turkish manner. Over his shirt he wore a gown (*casacha*) of yellow satin (*raso*) and over that one of damask with great flowers in gold thread. Over that he had one of scarlet.

Seated on a fine carpet, he must have looked quite a sight.

Female dress may also have been highly conservative, though the sixteenth- and seventeenth-century European costume books abound in depictions of peasant women in Anatolia, Thrace and the Greek Islands, all with marked local differences. Much later, Mouradjea d'Ohsson, dragoman of the Swedish Embassy in Istanbul in the late eighteenth century, recorded his experiences there in his *Tableau Général de l'Empire Ottoman*; in this account he embarks on a tirade setting the fickleness of European fashion against the stability of the Ottomans:[5]

> Les modes qui tyrannisent tant l'esprit des femmes européennes n'agitent guères le sexe en Orient: là c'est presque toujours la même coëffure, la même coupe d'habits, le même genre d'étoffes. On ne doit point s'étonner de cette stabilité de la nation dans ses goûts et dans ses usages, puisque ni à Constantinople, ni dans aucune ville de l'Empire, on ne voit point de ces marchandes de modes intéressées à aiguilloner l'inconstance et la frivolité par la mobilité perpétuelle de leurs inventions.

Women are, however, rarely depicted in Ottoman illustrated works before 1700, and the earliest descriptions we have are likewise from this period, by which time female clothing might well have changed considerably from sixteenth-century norms. The earliest known to me, predating Lady Mary Wortley Montagu's much better known account (cf. p. 162) by more than forty years, is by Antoine Galland who, amusingly, was made to dress up to play the part of Elvire, the *confidante* of Chimène in Corneille's *Le Cid* for a performance at the French Embassy in Galata early in 1673.[6] His costume consisted of the usual baggy trousers, of striped tabby silk down to the ankles, and a fine cotton vest with wide sleeves which came quite low. Over this he wore a gown or a skirt of gold and silver brocade on a red ground with buttons of gold thread and narrow sleeves reaching to the wrist, where they were wrapped with double gold chains which served as bracelets. Over the gown was a silk kaftan in beige (*feuille morte claire*) with gold lace buttons and a girdle of rubies and diamonds, but left open to show the vest beneath. On top he wore a red cloak (*ferāce*) lined with sables, which he also left open. No Ottoman Turks were invited to this performance. Had they attended and seen Galland all dressed up as a woman, they would doubtless have been much shocked by the spectacle.

D'Ohsson concedes[7] that despite the conservatism of Ottoman dress there was no absolute uniformity, since differences marked individuals from the various provinces of the Ottoman Empire, as well as the various classes and conditions of men. From the time of Süleymān the Magnificent, he claims, these social distinctions were announced increasingly by the wearing of particular turbans, partly because one Sultan after another in the early sixteenth century adopted his own form of turban, in size and shape, material, and also the colour and size of the skull-cap around which the turban cloth was wound. Though experiments in turbans were abandoned by officials by 1600, the Sultans continued to wear turbans in styles of their own choosing. That of Muṣṭafā III (1757–74) was particularly flamboyant, of white muslin and of enormous diameter, with a long plume and an aigrette of diamonds. Nevertheless, the European conviction that Fashion was absent as a factor in the development of Ottoman costume came to be shared by the Ottomans themselves. The memoirs of Shaykh Rifāʿa Rāfiʿ al-Ṭahṭawī (1801–73), who was sent by Muḥammad ʿAlī of Egypt to Paris in 1826 to study there, well express this:[8]

> One of the characteristics of the French is their avid curiosity for everything that is new and their love of change and variety in all things and especially in the matter of dress. This is never fixed with them and no fashion or adornment has remained with them till now. This does not mean that they change their dress entirely; it means that they vary it. Thus for example they would not stop wearing a hat and replace it by a turban, but they sometimes wear a hat of one kind and then after a while replace it with a hat of another kind, whether in shape or colour or the like.

To this one is inclined to reply that Shaykh Rifāʿa was a legal official and a member of the highly conservative *ʿulamā*; that the French were notorious for flightiness, as the English were in the early nineteenth century for melancholy or 'spleen'; and that conservatism in dress has always been a matter of pride, a 'Victorian value', even when the impact of fashion on the wearer has been quite marked. Nevertheless, there can be no doubt that European observers rightly contrasted the stability of Ottoman dress with the extravagance and search for novelty which characterize the evolution of upper-class dress in Renaissance and post-Renaissance Europe. This the late Fernand Braudel has attributed not to D'Ohsson's merchants and peddlers but to economic motives, notably conspicuous consumption to reinforce a dominant social or economic position, and partly to the constitution of post-medieval Europe in which national elements in upper-class dress had long had an important cultural role; partly also there was a constant drive for innovation, even improvement, which ultimately, in his view, is to be connected with the European discoveries in Africa and Asia, and even with the Industrial Revolution.

Put so baldly, this sort of explanation may well excite ridicule. But psychologies differ, and states differ, and it is not absurd to think of certain cultures as being more subject to the vagaries of Fashion than others. It would obviously be invidious to suggest which cultures are most liable to accept hairdressers as the stars of dinner parties, but there can be no doubt that their equivalent certainly attended Venetian banquets in the sixteenth century. At the same time European observers certainly exaggerated the differences; for, under the impact of severe sumptuary legislation in the sixteenth–seventeenth centuries, not even the richest merchants and noblemen of Venice or Florence could afford to throw aside their garments of brocade or cloth of gold in favour of post-Reformation black, which, if sober in appearance, was doubtless wildly expensive in cut. On the other hand, as in the later seventeenth and eighteenth centuries the Ottoman market became more and more open to European trade through the various Capitulations, the impact of rapidly changing European styles and patterns, from, for example, the Lyons silk factories, reflected strongly on the fabrics available for tailoring and very probably inspired the patterns of the *selīmīye* silks (*ills. 66–9*) woven in Istanbul.[10]

It could well be argued that in Europe the impact of sumptuary legislation, though, as in Ottoman Turkey, intended to enhance social as much as economic distinctions, was less severe because such regulations were less rigidly enforced.[11] Moreover, despite D'Ohsson's valiant assertion of the conservatism of Ottoman ladies' dress, Lady Mary Wortley Montagu's description of the costume she ordered for herself, no less than the 'fashion plates' of eighteenth-century beauties executed by Levnī, the Court Painter (*naḳḳāşbaşı*)[12] of Aḥmed III (1703–30), shows that her appreciation of the sexuality of the garments was not a distortion of their function. In contrast to this, however, the constant toying with sexuality, an obsession, even, with the masculinity or effeminacy of much Renaissance and post-Renaissance male costume seems utterly alien to the costumes and textiles of the Ottoman Empire. Fashion here seems to be an irrelevance: simply, to a far greater degree than in contemporary Europe Ottoman male clothing – underwear, dishabille and even clothing for sports or military exercises – was adapted as much to the requirements of hygiene and comfort as to outward show. Significantly also – with the exception of Selīm I (1512–20) who, despite his constant strife with the Safavids in Iran, like the Safavid Shah Ṭahmāsp shaved his beard – Ottoman hairdressing and the cut of the beard scarcely changed for three centuries, while Europe went through moustaches, ringlets, periwigs and much else. Only in the nineteenth century, when the Sultans and their courtiers turned to the discomfort of 'Victorian' Court dress, did they also take, more or less, to European styles of hairdressing.

This conservatism is doubtless the offspring of deeply rooted Muslim conceptions of decency and dignity in dress, even if the Sultans' taste for silks and gold went against the lawyers' deepest convictions concerning propriety. It was also reinforced by the hierarchy of robes appropriate to the various legal, military and administrative classes of Ottoman society. Since these garments were also part of the Ottoman honours system there was a constant conflict between considerations of expense and a concern that materials, tailoring and trimmings should not be debased. Either, however, was an inducement to conservatism. Whatever quibbles might arise, the fact remains that Ottoman official garments apparently evolved very little between 1550 and 1800.

In the case of kaftans made for Sultans, one might well object that this conclusion remains unproved. Unfortunately, too few of the surviving garments are attributable to a single Sultan or to successive Sultans for it to be possible to identify or evaluate changes in style. These certainly existed, however, as the history of costume in fifteenth-century Mamlūk Egypt, from which the Ottomans derived much of their ceremonial, amply demonstrates: here the trappings of Court ceremonial relating to the presentation of robes of honour were highly responsive to differences in cut. How these looked is now difficult to reconstruct, but Ottoman Treasury inventories like that of Bāyazīd II (1505)[13] contain numerous references to *Mīrāḫūrī* (one translates, in the style of the Constable, or Master of the Horse); *dūcevī* (a broad-sleeved garment worn oven a tunic or *duliman*, a calque from Venetian *dogale*); *Ḫazinedārī* and *Çāvūşī*, robes presented to officials or to individuals, including spies, who had deserved well of the Ottoman authorities.[14] Whatever they signified, these official styles were not the only garments on offer, and must have waxed and waned with the tastes of Ottoman Sultans from 1500 to 1800. Finally, although the tailoring of these garments is of the simplest, the presence of conspicuous collars on some kaftans (*ill. 44*), tailored rather than straight skirts (*ill. 32*) and marked differences in trimming and buttons of fronts and sleeves (*ills. 24, 55*) show that, in details at least, the tailoring of these kaftans was far from invariable. The history of Italian tailoring is traceable relatively easily through the numerous portraits of grandees from the Renaissance onwards. Even there, however, its details are largely a mystery;[15] it is not surprising, meanwhile, that it should be possible to conclude so little on the history of Ottoman ceremonial costume.

How willing Ottoman emissaries abroad were to dress up in European costume is difficult to decide. If to refuse to accept a robe of honour was dangerous in many later Islamic Courts, it would have been little less dangerous or embarrassing to refuse a European Renaissance robe – a serious gaffe, if not an outright insult. However, once the mission was safely back at home the robe could be discreetly discarded, or cut up and used for saddle-cloths, wrappers or religious vestments.[16] It is, nevertheless, well to recall the account in Marino Sanuto's *Diarii*[17] of the official reception of an Ottoman emissary in the Venetian Senate, which had ordered for him a robe of crimson velvet from the Republic's most expensive tailor. There is no reason to believe that Venetian tailors should not have been able to make up an Ottoman-style kaftan to the emissary's specifications, but although Marino Sanuto refers on other occasions to Ottoman officials in Venice wearing kaftans and tunics presented by the Signoria,[18] it remains possible that some Ottoman emissaries liked the idea of being dressed up as if in a portrait by Tintoretto. It is quite possible that, as Antoine Galland's escapade in playing a lady of mature years on the stage shows, dressing up was a peculiarly European pleasure; but for an Ottoman official a Venetian dress would have been extremely useful for espionage.

If the evident impact of Fashion on style and cut is difficult to evaluate, its role in the determination of design and pattern is, maddeningly, obscured by the absence of any fine chronology, the very small number of attributable silks and the extreme difficulty of identifying the types, patterns and even manufactures, which the documents all too rarely mention. On the one hand, there is the pervasive influence of Italian designs (*ills. 27, 28, 31*) and adaptations (*ills. 14, 29*), though the traffic from the Levant to Italy was evidently heavy enough to evoke Venetian embargoes against imported gold and silver brocades.[19] This suggests that many Venetian silks for the Levant must have been already orientalized,[20] for the sixteenth-century Ottoman documents mention flowered (*gulistānī*), patterned (*naḳışlı*) and spotted or speckled (*benek*) designs, and practically nothing else.

This last category seems to be a crux. It has generally been assumed that it refers to the triple-spot and tiger-stripe pattern which was extremely popular in Ottoman decoration in the late sixteenth century: on the basis of this identification, and the occurrence of the term for silks in the 1505 inventory of the Treasury of Bāyazīd II, a number of such kaftans have been attributed to Selīm I (*ill. 8*). The trouble is that *benek* seems to have been far too common merely to apply to a single design. Presents from Alvise Gritti to Pietro Zen in Istanbul in 1533[21] included robes of gold-brocaded velvet, of *benecchi d'oro*, and Persian or Oriental stuff (*a l'azemina*) made at Bursa. This, and the fact that there is a perfectly good word in Ottoman Turkish for leopard or leopard-spotted (*pelenk*)[22] suggest that in fact *benek* was a fairly general term for any medallion silk.

On the other hand, the preponderance of gold, crimson and yellow, of medallion or ogival patterns or of designs based on crescent or triple-spot motifs, and of filling motifs including foliate arabesques, chinoiserie cloud-scrolls and the mis-called 'quatre fleurs' (a wide repertory of florists' flowers) in silks of the later sixteenth century is certainly congruent with Court taste, even though the silks were ordered by or for private individuals or designed by specialist designers or mostly made outside Court manufactories. The designs therefore reflect Court fashion in decoration, and when that changes in the seventeenth century they change with it. Exceptionally, moreover, the resemblances are so close as to suggest that the Court actually employed a designer to adapt a favourite pattern to a textile, or vice versa. Such is the virtuoso brocade (*ill. 18*) which may be associated with the unfortunate Şehzāde Bāyazīd (strangled 1561) and which is remarkably close to blue-and-white tile panels, datable to c. 1560, on the façade of the Sünnet Odası (Circumcision Room) in the Topkapı Saray. Both must have been done from drawings or cartoons, though not from the same design. It is impossible to say, however, which was adapted from the other.

Some kaftans – evidently made for Sultans, even if the materials were not specially ordered by them – decorated with sunbursts and stars (*ill. 20*), and tailored so that the design appears absolutely symmetrical, suggest that the Ottoman rulers must have enjoyed looking like stage magicians in a pantomime – or possibly like Rudolf II's astrologers. One of this type, with dashing hexagrams and flowers, not illustrated here, has been attributed by Tahsin Öz[23] to Meḥmed II (1451–81), though the design is more appropriate to the later sixteenth century, and the sunburst patterns, in brocade or lamé in a more muted colour range, are more typically seventeenth century.

Though relations to precise tile patterns are exceptional, there is clearly a general relation between the designs of Bursa silks and Iznik tiles from *c.* 1560 onwards, where the use of bole red evokes the standard crimson ground of so many silks. The tiles, over a period of little more than forty years, were mass-produced in enormous quantities to decorate mosques and palaces built by the Sultans, their ladies and their viziers in Edirne and Istanbul. The records show, moreover, that in this case the central authorities constantly interfered, even if their references to *drawings* for tiles relate practically exclusively to inscriptions (at which the Iznik potters when left unsupervised were notoriously, if unaccountably, incompetent) and such official interference did not extend to ordering tiles of particular patterns for particular panels or friezes. The similarities of colour, allowing for technical limitations, and the widespread use of medallion or ogival designs for both tilework and textiles suggest strongly that the use of Iznik tilework in Ottoman architecture of the late sixteenth and the early seventeenth century was inspired by textile hangings. But, for several reasons, the results were independent adaptations. First, tile designs show greater freedom, for textile designs, particularly those with heavy metal thread, must take account of the resulting weight. Secondly, when worn or hung, even the heaviest, stiffest brocade will drape or assume a three-dimensional effect. This makes it appropriate to have denser, heavier designs for medallions which in tilework would be unbearably ponderous, repetitious or dull. In fact, no tile design exactly reproduces that of a textile: the balance of filling and ground is practically never the same; and tilework of the highest quality tends to turn from the use of repeating designs to discrete panels.

This is not to say that textile designs evolved without any control, entirely independently of the customer's taste, for there is, in the Armoury of the Moscow Kremlin,[24] a brocaded satin which was made up into a cope (*sakkos*) presented in 1583 to the Cathedral of the Dormition in Moscow by Ivan the Terrible in commemoration of his murdered son. Its design shows remarkable responsiveness to sectional demand, for the repeating pattern shows the Virgin and Child with angels, Greek crosses and wreaths of characteristically Ottoman florists' flowers, a striking adaptation of Bursa silk designs of the later sixteenth century to Byzantine iconography. Unlike many of the Bursa brocades in Russian cathedral treasuries, the cope was most probably made up from a loom-piece ordered for a church vestment and not cut down from an earlier Tsar's robe. When and how the silk reached Muscovy is not recorded, but the recent discovery in the Łwów archives, of a complaint by an unnamed Polish customer that an Ottoman merchant, Muṣliḥeddīn, or his Armenian interpreter, had sold the 'cross stuff' (*ḫāclū ḳumāş*) he had ordered to the governor of Łwów instead, and that the merchant was not to behave like this in future, shows that the fabric was almost certainly one of a group. The complaint is dated 1548.[25]

It is by no means surprising that the Orthodox priests (Russians or Greeks), whose presence in Bursa is attested from the late fifteenth century onwards, should have commissioned special silks from the Bursa weavers, some of whom may well have been Greek. More may well come to light therefore. But this is only one aspect of the powerful eclectic forces which governed sixteenth-century Ottoman taste. Another is shown by a remarkable letter in the Venetian archives dated Şevval 961/September 1554[26] from the Ottoman Beglerbeg of Egypt, Dekākīnzāde Meḥmed, to an old acquaintance in Venice, Propicia Mano, whom he had known when the latter was Venetian Bailo (Resident) in Aleppo, to say that he had had designs for silks drawn in Cairo to be woven in Venice. They had been despatched via the Venetian Bailo in Cairo, Daniele Barbarigo, but there was an inexplicable delay. Could his old friend look into the matter and speed things up? It is, of course, very difficult to determine from this what the design could have been, for it could well have been drawn by a Venetian or Spanish designer in Cairo; nor need it necessarily have been even hybrid European-Ottoman. The letter shows, however, the very close connections in taste and means that existed between high Ottoman officials and merchants or patricians in the Northern Mediterranean.

Notes to Chapter 5

1 *Dōlma* goes into both Italian (as *duliman*) and other European languages, but, typically, changes its sense. In Venetian it seems to be used both for the under-gown and the kaftan. In Hungarian usage it seems to be a short tunic, with long sleeves.

2 Topkapı Saray Archives, D.12a–b.

3 G. Fehér, *Craftsmanship in Turkish-ruled Hungary* (Budapest 1975), 32 and Pl. 3.

4 Marino Sanuto, *Diarii* LVI (1900–1), 742.

5 D'Ohsson, *Tableau Général de l'Empire Ottoman* IV (Paris 1791), 149.

6 Ch. Schéfer (ed.), *Journal d'Antoine Galland pendant son séjour à Constantinople* (Paris 1881) II, 14–16: 29 January 1673.

7 D'Ohsson, op. cit., 112–18.

8 *Takhlīṣ al-Ibrīz fī Talkhīṣ Barīz* (Cairo 1958); cited after Bernard Lewis, *The Muslim Discovery of Europe* (New York 1982).

9 *The Structures of Everyday Life. The Limits of the Possible*

(*Civilisation and Capitalism 15th–18th century*, Vol. I), trans. Siân Reynolds (London–New York 1981), 266–333.

10 There is in the Victoria and Albert Museum a pattern book (671.1919) with eighteenth-century Lyons silk-patterns in stripes and small floral repeating designs, with notes (in Ottoman Turkish phonetically transcribed into Greek) indicating the thread content by colour. It may have been intended for Ottoman clients to order designs to be woven for them in Lyons; but the notes suggest that the designs were to be copied locally by Ottoman weavers.

11 The series of large woodcuts published by the mid-sixteenth-century Venetian printer Mathio Pagan (Pagani) showing a procession in St Mark's Square, Venice, includes the ladies, who are seen watching it from the upper stories of the Procuratie (Nuove) dressed in finery which Venetian sumptuary regulations expressly forbade. *La processione del Doge nella Domenica delle Palme*. Facsimile (Venice 1880).

In Florence, successive laws were passed by Cosimo I (1546, 1562, 1568) limiting the use and wear of brocades, silks, furs, scents and trimmings, possibly with women principally in view; see R. Bonito-Fanelli, 'I drappi d'oro: Economia e moda a Firenze nel Cinquecento' in *Le Arti nel Principato Mediceo* (Florence 1980), 407–26. But numerous exceptions were permitted and Cesare Vecellio's *Habiti Antichi et Moderni di tutto il Mondo* (1st ed., Venice 1590) chooses as representative illustrations of Florentine costume individuals who are extremely richly dressed.

12 ʿAbd al-Jalīl, better known as Levnī, came from Edirne; his appointment dates from *c.*1720.

13 J. M. Rogers, 'An Ottoman palace inventory of the reign of Beyazid II', *VE^e Colloque du CIEPO, Cambridge 1984,* ed. J.-L. Bacqué-Grammont (Istanbul 1986).

14 The *dogale* or *ducale* was a wide-sleeved outer-garment worn over a *duliman* of crimson or cloth of gold, lined with white velvet for summer wear and with fine furs for the winter. Cf. Eugenio Albèri (ed.), *Le relazioni degli ambasciatori Veneti al Senato durante il secolo decimosesto* III/3 (Florence 1855), xix. In the Ottoman documents the term probably refers to the cut, rather than to the materials Albèri specifies. The account-books for Court expenditure in the year 909/1503–4 – see Ö. L. Barkan, 'Osmanlı saraylarına ait muhasebe defterleri', *Belgeler* IX (Ankara 1979), 296–380, Item 38 – list *Ḫazinedārī* and *Çāvūşī* robes among the rewards received by Şerefeddīn ʿAlī, who had presented a large carpet, evidently from a descendant of the Akkoyunlu rulers of Tabriz, to Bāyazīd II. The term used is *ʿādet*, which generally relates to customary gratuities: since, however, he was also given a large sum in cash, these robes must relate to uniforms, respectively, of a Treasury official and a military officer.

15 Cf. I. Petraschek-Heim, *Die Meisterstückbücher des Schneider-Handwerks in Innsbruck* (Innsbruck 1970).

16 For example, the Italian silks listed in the Court accounts of Bāyazīd II for the year 909/1503–4, most of which were made up as saddle-cloths (cf. note 14 above)

17 *Diarii* LIII (1899), 280, 20 June 1530: 'Viene l'orator del Signor turco, vestito di una vesta li ha fato la Signoria cernita per lui in casa di maistro Antonio di Moti il primo di tal mestier, et richissimo d'oro roso, et ruose verde, belisima a veder.'

18 *Diarii* XXIII (1888), 439. The envoy appeared at the Signoria wearing a crimson velvet kaftan (*caxacha*) with, under it, the white damask robe (presumably a Turkish *dōlma*) which the Signoria had presented to him.

19 Decree dated 4 May 1490, cf. F. Brunello, *Arti e Mestieri a Venezia nel medioevo e nel Rinascimento* (Vicenza 1981), 127.

20 A. J. B. Wace, 'The dating of Turkish velvets', *Burlington Magazine* LXIV (1934), 164–70.

21 Marino Sanuto, *Diarii* LVIII/1 (1901–3), 304.

22 A Palace register of 1525 (Topkapı Saray Archives, 732/5718) lists Bursa velvet with leopard spots (*pelenk*) in black, green and red, Bursa velvets with leopard spots in heavy gold embroidery (*zerbāft*), and green brocade with leopard spots in black. Tahsin Öz, who notes the reference (*Türk Kumaş ve Kadifeleri* II, 89), takes *pelenk* to mean tiger-stripes; but *pelenk* is not used for 'tiger' in the dictionaries.

23 Öz, ibid., I, Pl. ix.

24 A. A. Goncharova (ed.), *Gosudarstvennaya Oruzheinaya Palata Moskovskogo Kremlya* (Moscow 1969), No. 74.

25 Zygmunt Abrahamowicz, *Katalog dokumentów tureckich. Dokumenty do dziejów Polski i krajów ościennych w latach 1455–1672* (Warsaw 1959), 101, No. 96.

26 M. Tayyip Gökbilgin, 'Venedik Devlet Arşivindeki vesikalar külliyatında Kanunî Sultan Süleyman devri belgeleri', *Belgeler* I/2 (Ankara 1964), 219. The Venetian name is given phonetically in the Ottoman text and may well be corrupt.

6

Some sources for the history of Ottoman textiles

FOR the merchants of the trading cities of the Northern Mediterranean in the fifteenth and sixteenth centuries the markets of the Eastern Mediterranean were as rich as any in Northern Europe. This was not merely because the enormous consumption of oriental spices and drugs in Northern Europe gave the spice trade predominant importance in international commerce, but also because these markets furnished an essential outlet for European raw materials and manufactured goods. In Alexandria in the late fifteenth century, for example, the foreign trading establishments included Ragusan, Florentine, Genoese, Marseillais, Catalan and Aragonese, while Cairo, which was opened up to foreigners essentially in the period following Selīm I's conquest of Egypt in 1516–17, was soon swarming with European merchants too. That the trade continued and even increased indicates its economic importance and scale: for it was not only vulnerable to the fluctuations of Ottoman policy; it was also at the mercy of European wars, civil disturbances and, for short periods at least, Papal embargoes.

Not surprisingly, the documentary material for the textile trade on the European side, though fragmentary and scattered, is rich and various. It includes Chancery rescripts conferring or requesting commercial privileges; manuals of customs and other dues to be paid at various Mediterranean ports; lists of presents offered by envoys; travel accounts, by merchants or pilgrims; merchants' account books or archives; and inventories drawn up on confiscation or decease, for the benefit of the authorities or the heirs. Like their Ottoman counterparts, they mostly have some disadvantages, though their varied nature and the useful fact that often the European and the Ottoman sources complement one another make individual shortcomings less important for the general picture.

Chancery rescripts are sometimes only of incidental value, for they rarely go into details of the goods in question. An exception is a Mamlūk complaint dated 10 Şevvāl 877/1 January 1473 NS[1] that Venetian merchants were foisting poor-quality woollen cloth upon the Alexandria market; that they were giving short measure – 30-ell instead of the customary 55-ell pieces; and that their brocades were counterfeit, being of gilt copper, not gold, thread.[2] This is some evidence that the Mamlūks, like the Ottomans, controlled the quality of goods sold in the market, but it is far less informative than the list of presents, mentioned as being attached to the document but now lost, would have been. As for the Italian manuals of customs dues, port charges, lading costs and cargo lists, they tend to lump cloths under broad headings which give little idea of their quality or even of the quantities in which they were exported. Secondly, they are mostly occasional collections of miscellaneous information for merchants trading with the Levant and circulated in numerous editions, generally without any revision. Admittedly, they never became entirely useless, because of periodical inelasticities of supply and demand in European trade with the East; but, notoriously, Balduccio Pegolotti's *Pratica della Mercatura*, which by the time he came to compile it (*c.* 1340) was already more than fifty years out of date, was substantially repeated in the late fifteenth century in Francesco Borlandi's *El libro di mercatantie et usanze de' paesi*, and even later in Pagnini della Ventura's *Della Decima*,[3] by which time the content was obviously totally anachronistic.[4]

The difficulties presented by these manuals are further compounded by the regular use of Oriental names for stuffs, quite irrespective of their place of manufacture: thus, for example, the use of the terms damask, tabby and samite for fabrics made in Europe was no guarantee of similarity.[5] Even when weavers were concerned to imitate, there were good imitations as well as bad, improvements as well as tawdry experiments. Patents did not exist, and the same term was often used for certain textile types, whatever their provenance; and since different centres rarely specialized in textiles of a single type, the name of the centre was often preserved in examples of textiles of quite different types woven over a long period of time. There is, for example, Marco Polo's report[6] that *mosulin*

(Italian, *mossorini*) was woven at Mosul, referring, however, not to the fine cottons we know as muslins, but to a cloth of silk and gold. It is possible that the text is corrupt; but there are many other documented cases where the same name for a fabric covers both silk and cotton or woollen materials. Thus, it follows that, even when we can discover what material was made where, we still have practically no idea of its appearance and not necessarily even an idea of what it was made of. This situation makes it very difficult to evaluate the sources when it comes to speaking of the influence that one weaving centre may have had upon another. It may be more than a curiosity, however, that whereas both the Italian and the Ottoman sources refer to various textile types being made at Bursa – lampas, tabby, damask, satin, samite, etc. – Bursa itself, notwithstanding this fatal tendency for textiles to be named after places, never gave its name to a particular fabric.

Merchants' account books are in essence more informative, but their relevance depends to a large extent on the merchant's own spheres of interest. Thus the Archivio Datini at Prato,[7] an irreplaceable source for both quantities and quality of exports in the Tuscan woollen trade with Northern Europe and with Catalonia, is, to judge from published documents, of much less value for trade with the Levant. And the Fuggers, who for much of the sixteenth century, kept a permanent office in Istanbul, seem to have concentrated on banking, to the total exclusion of imports and exports. Travellers' and pilgrims' accounts are also only of incidental value, largely because they not only tended to follow a set route – Istanbul, Aleppo, Palestine, Sinai, Cairo and Alexandria (sometimes in the reverse order) – but also because clearly guidebooks for pilgrims were available (though not, unfortunately, of Baedeker quality) from which it was far more practical to copy out passages verbatim to puff a narrative, rather than keep a daybook and use their own eyes. Or else their dragomans were as repressive as modern tourist-guides and remorselessly repeated the same set of clichés for each set of newcomers: original observations of any kind, not just those relating to textile manufacture and sale, are few and far between. This is unfortunately also true of the European attachés to the Habsburg embassies to Ottoman Turkey of the mid- and later sixteenth century, even though internal political conditions made it very much easier for them to travel.

The great exception to these regrettably negative remarks is the *Diarii* of Marino Sanuto who, from *c.* 1490 to 1533, was the secretary of the Venetian Council of Ten. They consist variously of: political despatches from all over Europe and the Levant; *Relations* by Venetian envoys on their return from a mission; shipping movements and bills of lading; and detailed, graphic accounts of legislation of all sorts and of the daily life of the Venetian patricians, including processions on feast days, audiences to foreign envoys and lists of their gifts. By an extremely fortunate coincidence, moreover, the contents of the *Diarii* cover a period, embracing the reigns of Bāyazīd II and Selīm I and the early part of the reign of Süleymān the Magnificent, from which a series of inventories, account books and registers of craftsmen woking in the Palace have been preserved, making it possible to complement or to check Sanuto's narrative. Some of his sources have their drawbacks. In particular, ambassadors' *Relations* – discourses on the geography, politics, manners and customs of the lands they have visited – were first and foremost exercises for the entertainment of the Venetian Senate, and tend to repeat one another and consist as much of pompous generalization as of telling details. But they were, like the Ottoman bureaucrats with whom they talked and corresponded, interested in the details of the conduct of diplomatic relations.[8] Hence, the great variety of Marino Sanuto's source-material, his central position in the Venetian Chancery and his own powers of observation and description make the *Diarii* a document that is constantly worth citing. Though they could, obviously, be amplified by recourse to European and Ottoman archives there is little of substance they seem to have omitted.

The documentary sources, then, though abundant, are not always helpful. They are sometimes no better informed than we ourselves are and at the worst convey too well the ignorance and confusion which surrounds the history of textiles from the fifteenth to the eighteenth century in Europe and the Eastern Mediterranean. Nor are the pictorial sources invariably more useful. The illustrated Ottoman chronicles of the later sixteenth century have now been recognized as invaluable sources for the daily life of the Sultans and also of the Palace.[9] Nevertheless, even Loqmān's *Ḳiyāfetü'l-Insānīye*, *c.* 1579 (Topkapı Saray Library, H.1563), the avowed aim of which was the accurate depiction of the Ottoman Sultans,[10] rarely shows them in patterned robes and even more rarely suggests robes which are extant in the Topkapı Saray collections today. Exceptionally, however, a sable-lined brocade kaftan in the Topkapı Saray collections (No. 31/932),[11] does correspond satisfactorily to that depicted in a well-known portrait of Selīm II (1566–74) by Ḥaydār Reīs (Nigārī) showing him practising archery (Topkapı Saray Library, H.2134/3).[12]

On the European side, particularly Northern Europe and North Italy, one might expect considerable information from painters, who had a well established tradition of accurately depicting brocades and velvets in paintings,[13] either for garments or as a foil to the figures – one thinks of the Bronzino portrait of Eleanor of Toledo (1546), in the Uffizi in Florence, with the Spanish or Italian brocaded velvet dress in which she was indeed clad after her death. In sixteenth-century Venice there was particular interest in depictions of the Ottoman Sultans. Titian, for example, is reported to have painted no fewer than four pictures of Süleymān the Magnificent,[14] though none has survived. None of these paintings can have been from the life and some were highly imaginative. As a result there was not the same compulsion to paint their robes exactly; or painters preferred to copy engraved portraits of varying freedom rather than to scour the Venetian markets for plausible Bursa silks.

Among the large-format North Italian prints of the sixteenth century (mostly anonymous Venetian, more or less associated with the circle of Titian) is a set of prints issued and probably engraved by the publisher Domenico de' Franceschi,[15] showing Süleymān riding in the customary Friday procession to the mosque in Istanbul, with his viziers, the *ʿulamā'* and Janissary units. This is, by contrast, no imaginary scene, but must have been drawn from the life: in this case some of the kaftans shown are practically identical in pattern to examples still in the Topkapı Saray collection (*ill. 51*). This verisimilitude is all the more remarkable since foreigners seen sketching in Ottoman Istanbul were very liable to be arrested as spies, so that the sketches must have been very hasty and would have needed to be worked up from memory in the safety of a foreign embassy, without recourse to the actual procession, or, even later, back in Venice. In the latter case of course, the rendering of the textiles could have been corrected by reference to garments worn by an Ottoman emissary.

Elsewhere in Europe, or in Istanbul for other foreign envoys, the later sixteenth century shows a vogue for Turkish costume books. Some were bazar art, lacking in detail as well as ability, but among the rest were the illustrations to Siegmund von Herberstein's *Relation* of his travels to Istanbul and to Muscovy as the Habsburg Emperor's ambassador. This work contains a picture of him wearing the kaftan (which, to judge from the pattern, must have been a Venetian velvet or brocade) presented to him by Süleymān the Magnificent, as well as others showing an interesting collection of embroidered and appliqué leather boots, weapons, etc. which he evidently acquired on his travels.[16] Also important are the illustrations to the *Relation* of the French traveller, Nicolas de Nicolay, published in 1567.[17] A hand-coloured copy in the British Library (C.55 i.4) includes two plates showing respectively a Jewish girl from Edirne (*ein Jüdische Jungfrau zu Adrianopel*) and a low Turkish woman (*ein Türckin schlechtes stands inn irer Haus Kleidung*) – respectable Ottoman ladies would not have been a subject for European travellers to see and sketch in the streets – both wearing elaborately patterned gowns, distinctly reminiscent of the kaftans associated with Şehzāde Muṣṭafā or Şehzāde Bāyazīd, the sons of Süleymān the Magnificent (*ill. 18*). The similarity is highly unexpected and should doubtless not be pressed: it is, for example, unclear how virtuoso brocades woven for princes should find their way to low women or to non-Muslims. But these illustrations do show that some European travellers properly appreciated the importance of luxury textiles in the life of the Ottoman ruling classes.

The pictorial evidence in European costume books should probably be followed up. Even more important from the documentary point of view, however, are textiles and embroideries which found their way to Eastern Europe, particularly to Hungary, which by the sixteenth century had become an Ottoman colony from the point of view of taste, and the semi-independent principalities of Transylvania, Moldavia and Wallachia. Veronika Gervers has well said:[18]

> At the height of Ottoman power in the 16th and 17th centuries interest in oriental garments was spread throughout the west by a general exotic trend in European fashionable costume. During the period the popularity of Turkish garments was in accord with the tendencies of Western modes. Yet if Turkish styles found a fertile ground in the Balkan countries, it was not primarily because of the parallel development in European fashion or because of an attraction to oriental splendour and luxury. The fact was that, as these territories became more and more isolated from the rest of Europe under the supremacy of the Sublime Porte, it was natural that costume and the minor arts should reflect the political context in which they took place.

In these areas it was not just that tribute was recognized by the Ottoman authorities by the standard presents of textiles, garments, and horse trappings: the presents catered to an established taste.

Further afield, Poland and Muscovy, though independently, had long had commercial connections with Ottoman Turkey and their merchants frequented Ankara, Bursa and Istanbul, trading the Northern products (see Chapter 9) in which they had control, wax, furs, amber and morse-ivory, for raw silk dyestuffs and spices. By the later sixteenth century, Bursa silks were much in demand for Tsars' garments and for ecclesiastical vestments, though whether they were woven on Palace looms in Istanbul or bought on the open market in Bursa is unclear. The rich remains of these are now in the Oruzheinaya Palata (the Armoury) in the Moscow Kremlin, the earliest datable pieces being mostly *c.* 1570–1600.[19] The earliest silks in Poland also seem to date from the same period. Virtually all the surviving pieces have been made up as church vestments.[20]

Even more widespread were the bolster-covers, velvet or brocade wrappers or bags for important documents, and embroidered saddles that were regularly presented to diplomatic missions to Istanbul or sent with Ottoman envoys and which still cram Royal armouries present and past in Stockholm, Moscow, Leningrad and Vienna.[21] These were considerably augmented by the spoils (*Türkenbeute*) from the series of defeats of the Ottoman armies by German and Austrian coalitions following the Relief of Vienna by John Sobieski in 1683. Like the fine appliqué and embroidered tents which were also captured, these go beyond the scope of the present volume. It should, however, be remembered that quite a lot of these spoils, unlike the diplomatic gifts, were already old when they were seized, so that the chronology of their style is quite probably complex.

This brief survey has been intended to show that European source material has been relatively little exploited up to the present for the chronology and provenance of much of the textile material in the Topkapı Saray collection. If further progress is to be made in their identification and attribution, however, it is these sources which offer the most promising prospects.

It remains to consider briefly the extant textiles dating from the pre-Ottoman and early Ottoman periods in Anatolia which, documentary evidence notwithstanding, are few and far between. There are two surviving silks which may be associated with Seljuk Anatolia. One, in the Musée Historique de Tissus in Lyons (23475 [881 IV 1]),[22] is a roundel brocade with lions and an almost illegible Arabic dedication inscription in the name of ʿAlā al-Dīn Kayqubād b. Kaykhusraw, one of the Seljuk Sultans of Konya. This has generally been taken to be Kayqubād I (1219–37), but recourse to the inscription reveals the further word *burhān* (the evident proof), part of a standard Seljuk title indicating the Sultan's standing vis-à-vis the ʿAbbāsid Caliphate in Baghdad, from which the Seljuks in Anatolia took their title to reign. *Burhān* comes rather low on the list of such titles, and Kayqubād I in fact used *qasīm* (equal partner): by elimination the Kayqubād must therefore be an epigone, Kayqubād II (1249–57). The only comparable silk is fragments of brocade, in the Kunstgewerbemuseum in West Berlin and in the treasury of the church of St Servatius in Siegburg,[23] with eagles and with dragons' heads. The design is stylistically close enough to much thirteenth-century Seljuk decoration to exclude European manufacture. But whether either or both were woven in Anatolia and in which city the looms were located remains an open question.

For the fourteenth century the extant material is even less impressive, though it is possible that further investigations in East European monastic treasuries and museum collections will bring to light parallels to the pall or funerary veil from the monastery of Studenica in Serbia.[24] This is a striped brocade bearing an inscription in the name of Sulṭān Bāyazīd Khān, hence either Bāyazīd I (1389–1402) or Bāyazīd II (1481–1512). Stylistically, it is difficult to say, but the close connections that existed between the Ottomans and the princes of Serbia in the late fourteenth century and the events following the crushing defeat of Serbia at the battle of Kosovo in 1389, which put an end to Serbian independence for several centuries, argue strongly for Bāyazīd I (Yıldırım). Dating from almost a century later, a pall in the monastery of Poutna in Romania[25] has evoked attention for its associations with Ottoman expansion in the Black Sea. This is a pall or tomb-cover of Maria of Mangop, the daughter of the Palaeologan prince of Mangop in the Crimea which fell into Ottoman hands shortly after the capture of Kaffa by Meḥmed II in 1475. The pall is of red silk with heavy gold embroidery representing the dead queen in her State robes, and on the basis of Maria of Mangop's Palaeologan descent has been claimed to be a church embroidery saved from the sack of Constantinople in 1453 and brought with her as part of her dowry. If it was liturgical, however, she would scarcely have worn it as a robe, and in fact the pattern is typical of 'ferronerie' Venetian velvets of the later fifteenth century. Its importance here is that it may be a depiction of a velvet made not in Venice but at Kaffa, which is documented in fifteenth- and sixteenth-century sources as being a velvet-weaving centre that produced fabrics highly esteemed in both Mamlūk Egypt and Ottoman Turkey but which so far have not been identified in any extant textiles.

These Eastern European embroidered Royal palls, halfway between carved Western effigies and the non-figural silks used in Ottoman Istanbul as tomb-covers, were a well established tradition and the silk fabrics they depict are thus valuable contributions to their chronology. That of the Moldavian prince Ieremia Movila (1596–1606)[26] from the monastery of Sucevița (Moldavia) shows him in a moiré robe with a rich long-sleeved, fur-lined kaftan over it, with a design of undulating stems of feathery lotuses and leaves. Allowing for slight distortions in the transfer into gold and silver embroidery, the pattern is that of a Bursa brocade which the embroiderer must have had before him as he worked.

There are two reasons why so few Ottoman silks from the fifteenth and early sixteenth centuries have survived. Up to the Fall of Constantinople in 1453, the Ottomans' imperial ambitions had been little more than a dream. The Conquest, however, made them heirs to the Byzantine emperors with, among their other deeply implanted traditions, the cult of imperial magnificence in silks and gold.[27] Yet, even when their means and their achievements might have justified it, their desire for rich garments faced the disapproval of nearly all the legal schools of Islam, which condemned the use of silk for hangings, furnishings and garments for adult males – unless, for example, the wearer suffered from lice (which, apparently, do not take well to silk clothing). So long as the Ottoman Sultans conceived themselves as the heirs to the Ottoman tradition of frontier warriors, magnificent costumes on a large scale were unthinkable, and the custom of having silks woven at or for the Court, for rulers, officials and for robes of honour, must be the result of a deliberate policy adopted by the Ottoman authorities. This result shows itself particularly in the mid- and later sixteenth century.

Recent research on the bindings of manuscripts in the Topkapı Saray Library has, unexpectedly, made considerable additions to our knowledge of fifteenth-century textiles.[28] The doublures (and occasionally the outer covers too) of a number of Mamlūk, Turcoman and Ottoman manuscripts have been discovered to be silk, sometimes in pristine condition, and since most of the texts they enclose have dated colophons, these establish a useful terminus for the binding: for the most part they are obviously contemporary with the manuscripts. Some of the silks (variously, satins, damasks and brocade) are Mamlūk, some Italian and some, possibly, even Chinese. Yet others are difficult to attribute exactly. But a narrow-striped crimson and blue silk covering the flap of the binding of a treatise on philosophy by Naṣīr al-Dīn Ṭūsī (A.3220) made for Meḥmed II and with a colophon dated 871/1466–7 is almost certainly Ottoman. And a doublure of deep-pink satin with an ogival pattern of linked palmettes in bright yellow (A.2460), on a manuscript datable to the late fifteenth century, shows how a design of typically Northern Italian origin was being adapted to Ottoman taste under Bāyazīd II. There are too few to hazard a guess at the most popular textile designs and types of this period; but it seems clear that the characteristic Bursa and Istanbul medallion designs of the later sixteenth century are a distinct development.

Notes to Chapter 6

1 S. Y. Labib, 'Ein Brief des Mamlukensultans Qā'itbey an den Dogen von Venedig', *Der Islam* XXXII (1957), 324–9; J. Wansborough, 'A Mamluk letter of 877/1473', *Bulletin of the School of Oriental and African Studies of the University of London* XXIV (1961), 200–13. Venice, Archivio di Stato, Ferrari, Documenti Turchi, Busta 15.

2 Francesco Borlandi's *El libro di mercatantie et usanze de' paese*, ed. F. Patetta and M. Chiaudano (Turin 1936), also refers *passim* to the risk of debased gold thread. I have not come across any Renaissance treatise, however, describing the possible sorts of inferior metal thread. Cennino Cennini's *Libro dell'Arte* – translated and ed. D. V. Thompson, Jr, as *The Craftsman's Handbook* (Yale University Press 1933; Dover, New York 1954), 107–8, 115–18 – does, however, treat of block-printing in gold to imitate damasks or brocades or even as a means of decorating velvet (of which Cennini can have seen little). The resultant fabric suggests a technique similar to that used for the silver-printed kaftan shown in ill. 26, though it must have been more suitable for furnishing than for wear.

3 *Della decima e dell'altre gravezze della moneta e della mercatura dei Fiorentini al secolo XVI* (Lisbon-Lucca 1775–6).

4 P. Grierson, 'The coin list of Pegolotti', in *Studi in Onore di Armando Sapori* I (Milan 1957), 485–92, is harsh and compelling: 'It was, however, very far from containing the 'cose bisognevoli di sapere a mercatanti di diverse parti del mondo' . . . and to a Florentine of *c.* 1340 the gaps in it must have been so enormous as to render it virtually useless. Its contents raise the suspicion that the *Pratica della Mercatura* is not so much the practical handbook of a man of business as a compilation of the notes which a retired merchant has at one time or another copied out in the hope that they would some day be useful and which now, in his old age, he cannot bring himself to jettison.

5 Borlandi's *El libro di mercatantie* (cited note 2 above) shows that, interestingly, European woollen cloths were clearly distinguishable from one another, in quality if not in weave, and, although there must have been numerous imitations, are identified mainly as the products of certain centres rather than as textile types. It is evident, however, from the lexical work of Francisque Michel – *Recherches sur le commerce, la fabrication et l'usage des étoffes de soie, d'or, d'argent et d'autres tissus précieux en Occident, principalement en France, pendant le Moyen Age* I-II (Paris 1852–4) – that from the fourteenth century onwards Lucca, then Venice, Florence, Siena and Genoa (the looms of which cities held the highest reputation for silks all over Europe, and much of the Near East too) were all identifying their fabrics in terms derived from oriental place-names. Paradoxic-

ally, however, *'alessandrino'* when applied to silks seems to refer not to Alexandria or to textiles made there, but to fabrics dyed with litmus or archil, in a colour something between azure and violet; cf. G. Gargiolli, *L'Arte della Seta in Firenze, Trattato del secolo XV* (Florence 1868), s.v. *'colore d'oricello'*.

6 P. Pelliot, *Notes on Marco Polo* II (Paris 1963), 783–5: 'Mosul'.

7 Cf. E. Ashtor, 'Les lainages dans l'Orient médiéval', *Atti della seconda settimana di studio, Istituto F. Datini* (Florence 1976), 657–86. The Bembo papers – cf. F. Thiriet, 'Les lettres commerciales des Bembo et le commerce vénitien dans l'Empire Ottoman à la fin du XVe siècle', in *Studi in Onore di Armando Sapori* II (Milan 1957), 913–33 – also appear to concentrate very much on wholesale trade with Istanbul, or with imports of wine and grain from the Morea, Negroponte and Candia to the Republic of Venice. However, the inventory of the estate of Giovanni di Francesco Maringhi, the Florentine draper who died in Galata in 1506 – cf. G. R. B. Richards, *Florentine merchants in the age of the Medici* (Cambridge, Mass. 1932), 184–201 – lists among his effects 'narrow silks' (sc. Italian silks, loom pieces in stock): *satins* – crimson, pink, pale yellow (*limonzino*) and blue, figured white, dark tan, figured green, plain green, tan and orange; *gold brocade*; *damasks* – crimson, green, *limonzino*, black, blue, green and tan; *velvets* – crimson and black. The woollens included Florentine cloth, made of Spanish wool; 'Levant' cloths (possibly stamped in Galata or Ragusa); and five iron presses for mohair or camlets.

8 Cf. an anonymous *Relation* of Süleymān's Persian campaign of 1553: 'In Aleppo l'arte della seta è grande, e bella, e si fanno velluti cremesini, panni d'oro bellissimi, e di seta, lavorati di più colori, e in copia grande, e laborati meglio di quelli che in altre parti si fanno', cited in Eugenio Albèri, *Relazioni degli ambasciatori veneti al Senato*, Series IIIa/I (Florence 1840) I, 224.

9 Nurhan Atasoy, 'The documentary value of the Ottoman miniatures' in *IVème Congrès International d'Art Turc* (Aix-en-Provence 1976), 11–17.

10 Seyyid Loqmān was appointed *şehnāmecı* (official annalist) in 1569 by Murād III.

11 *The Anatolian Civilisations*, exhibition catalogue (Istanbul 1983), E 106.

12 Ibid., E 107.

13 The work of Brigitte Klesse – *Seidenstoffe in der italienischen Malerei des vierzehnten Jahrhunderts* (Berne 1967) – shows how fruitful fourteenth-century painting has been for the chronology and distribution of both European and Eastern silks. For the subsequent period (1400–1600) Northern European painting, Flemish and German, is as important as Italian, but the enormous mass of material may have discouraged anyone from following her splendid example. The result is that the overall surveys are sketchy, as well as out of date, and detailed studies are of isolated groups. Cf. R. Grönwoldt, 'Notes on Italian and Spanish textiles of the seventeenth century' in Veronika Gervers (ed.), *Studies in Textile History in Memory of Harold B. Burnham* (Royal Ontario Museum, Toronto 1977), 126–32.

14 H. Wethey, *The Paintings of Titian. II. The Portraits* (London 1971).

15 Facsimile privately printed (Florence and Edinburgh 1877) for Sir William Stirling Maxwell as *Solyman the Magnificent going to Mosque*, from a series of engravings on wood published by Domenico de' Franceschi at Venice in MDLXIII.

16 Siegmund von Herberstein, *Actiones* (Vienna 1560); cf. Jennifer Wearden, 'Siegmund von Herberstein: an Italian velvet in the Ottoman Court', *Costume*, no. 19 (1985), 22–30.

17 This circulated all over Europe in numerous translations. The present copy is *Der Erste Theil von der Schiffart und Raiss in die Türckey und gegen Orient beschriben durch H. Niclas Nicolai, Kämmerling und Geographum des Künnigs inn Frannckreich* (1572).

18 *The Influence of Ottoman Turkish textiles and costume in Eastern Europe* (Royal Ontario Museum, Toronto 1982), 12.

19 The most recent catalogue is *Sokrovishcha prikladnogo iskusstva Irana i Turtsii iz sobraniya Gosudarstvennykh muzeyev Moskovskogo Kremlya*, exhibition catalogue (Moscow 1979).

20 These are mostly now in the National Museum in Warsaw; cf. *Tkanina turecka XVI-XIX w. ze zbiorów polskich*, exhibition catalogue (National Museum, Warsaw 1983).

21 Objects from these collections have been frequently published, but generally unsystematically and in inaccessible periodicals. One of the most useful publications relates to a series of bags and wrappers (*bohça*) in which State correspondence from the Sublime Porte was wrapped before despatch to Sweden. The oldest of these Swedish documents is late sixteenth century, most being seventeenth century or later. The bags or wrappers were mostly of unpatterned cloth of gold (*serāser*) or crimson satin, the type of material doubtless being strictly in accord with protocol. It is also possible that moiré taffeta or satin bags for State correspondence from the Ottomans to the Tatar Khāns of the Crimea are of Ottoman origin. Cf. Agnes Geijer and C. J. Lamm, *Orientalische Briefumschläge in schwedischem Besitz* (Stockholm 1944).

22 *The Anatolian Civilisations*, op. cit., D 175b.

23 Ibid., D 175a.

24 R. Ettinghausen, 'An early Ottoman textile', *First International Congress of Turkish Art. Communications presented to the Congress* (Ankara 1961), 134–40.

25 O. Tafrali, *Le trésor byzantin et roumain du monastère de Poutna* (Paris 1925), 51–6, Pl. XLIII.

26 Veronika Gervers (ed.), op. cit. (note 13 above), 84, Fig. 1.

27 R. Lopez, 'Silk industry in the Byzantine Empire', *Speculum* XX (1945), 1–15.

28 Zeren Tanındı, 'Cilt sanatında kumaş', *Sanat Dünyamız* Year 11, no. 32 (1985), 27–34.

7

Hierarchies and rank

On one thing travellers and ambassadors to Ottoman Turkey concur, that, in public at least,[1] only the Sultan or, at his express orders, one of his viziers could wear cloth of gold (*serāser*). Süleymān the Magnificent, as described by a Venetian emissary in 1532, when the Sultan was already in early middle age, must have looked resplendent, mounted on a fine white Turkish steed and wearing a long kaftan, cut slim, with long sleeves slit to the elbow, all of cloth of gold, over a *dolimano* or gown of crimson satin (*raso*) embroidered with large gold flowers, and with a belt of gold set with rubies and sapphires of inestimable value.[2] Even this apparel sounds less spectacular, however, than another Venetian report of Süleymān's and his viziers' dress:[3] 'The Sultan wears cloth of gold, whereas his predecessors wore camlet or mohair. Ibrāhīm Paşa [who was disgraced and executed in 1536] wears however, at the Sultan's express wish, gold brocade, and on campaign a suit of cloth of gold.' The implication throughout is that he eclipses the Sultan.

This evidence suggests that the limits to conspicuous consumption in public were set by the Sultan and his officials. Particularly interesting, therefore, is a long list of presents offered to Selīm I in Cairo in 1518 by two Venetian ambassadors, Bartolo Contarini and Alvise Mocenigo, ostensibly to congratulate him on the conquest of Egypt but doubtless also to secure commercial privileges for Venice.[4] It is too long to give complete, but the presents were, in descending order, to: the Sultan; his three viziers; his two Commanders-in-Chief and their respective Head Doorkeepers (Kapıcıbaşı) or chamberlains; the Chief Accountant (Defterdār) of Anatolia – the report states that his counterpart, the Defterdār of Rumeli, was not in Egypt; a high Chancery official, the Nişancıbaşı; the Commander of the Janissaries; the Sultan's tutor (Hoca); the military judge (Kazasker) of Rumeli or Thrace; the Master of the Horse (Imrāḫōr), the Sultan's Chamberlain (Kapıcıbaşı); other officers; the Dragoman; various local Egyptian officials who had deserved well of the Venetians; scribes and guards. All these (except for the Sultan and his viziers) have numerous deputies and 'friends' who receive, more or less, the presents appropriate to their bosses. To the Sultan the gifts were eight suits of the heaviest cloth of gold; one of crimson pile on pile velvet (*alto basso*); one of purple (*paonazo*) pile on pile; two of patterned (*coloradi*) pile on pile; one of plain crimson velvet and two patterned; two of crimson damask and eight patterned; two of crimson satin and eight patterned; and twenty scarlet; and twenty *paonazi* (purple, these probably wool also). The only official to receive cloth of gold, apart from the Sultan, was his tutor. Among the others the Chief Accountant did well with purple (*paonazo*) gold brocade, but the scale rapidly went down to the lowest officials, who were given damask and scarlet or purple cloth, some of it, quite probably, not garments but loom-pieces. The lowest, the 'friends' of the servants, are simply offered woollen cloth from Vicenza, which was well-known as a source of mediocre woollens.

This immensely long list of officials and their deputies, even quite minor deputies, strongly suggests that the Venetian ambassadors were under pressure from the chamberlains who received them to be free with their gifts. Though the stuffs, in descending order, show partly the value the Venetians put upon the stuffs and garments they presented, they also indicate their relative value in Ottoman estimation; and, although very little is known of the way in which such embassies actually worked, those which arrived without acceptable presents were promptly given to understand that they must find something suitable. The additional complication of such all-round gifts must have been that the ambassadors had to judge what was regarded as appropriate in the eyes of upper grades as presents to lower grades. Too little and the lower grades would have been offended; too much and their superiors would have resented it. There was no place for individual merit, so that the gifts were offered, and accepted, purely as hierarchical, as appropriate to the rank of the recipient. Otherwise, foreigners' missions would simply have been conducive to bad blood.

Such hierarchies were not, of course, an Ottoman invention. They must have been present at any European Court. But if an Eastern Mediterranean origin for the Ottomans' categorization of foreign gifts should be necessary, Mamlūk Egypt in the fourteenth and fifteenth centuries undoubtedly provided it. The mid-fourteenth-century writer on Chancery practice, al-ʿUmarī, who was summarized by several fifteenth-century Egyptian writers, gives wonderfully detailed lists of social and political distinctions to be observed in the presentation of robes of honour,[5] the value of which could, obviously, be considerably increased by lining or trimming with beaver or with squirrel fur. Not all the specifications have been fully elucidated, but the highest emirs were rewarded with crimson *Rūmī* (Anatolian, Turkish, Thracian, Byzantine – any of these descriptions might fit) satin, lined with golden yellow satin. Lesser mortals received: silk fabrics woven in the State factories of Egypt; velvets or brocades (possibly of Italian manufacture); and for the lowest or least deserving there were plain silk or even woollen stuffs. For viziers the most splendid robe, evidently made for investitures, was of white velvet or damask (*kamkhā*) with bands of embroidery in plain silk and lavish fur trimmings and lining; junior officials in the Chancery were presented with green brocade and such like.

For decades, even centuries, it must have been difficult to construe these occasional presentations of robes, however, stereotyped, as *uniforms*, though to the Egyptian officials and their Ottoman successors it must have been intolerable that anyone should wear a robe to which he was not entitled. Moreover, the differences in style and cut of the robes offered would plainly have counted, in terms of universal acceptance, toward the honour bestowed. But, inevitably, with time these robes became a mere ritual, and the regulations for dress on the formal reception of foreign ambassadors at the Ottoman Court in the eighteenth century show that required apparel was much the same as the uniforms or Court dress worn at any contemporary Court in Europe.[6]

The stuffs of hierarchy are well enough described. What they looked like is, unfortunately, another matter. One exceptional, though very puzzling, indication of designs of silk garments offered relates to the reward to Khayrbek (Muḥarram 925/January 1519), the Ottomans' Lieutenant in Egypt, though he had been overlooked by the Venetians in Cairo the previous year (see note 4); in this instance velvet with, of all things, a pattern of crocodiles (*tamāsīḥ*) on a crimson ground was used, and this, the contemporary Cairene chronicler Ibn Iyās implies,[7] had some sort of official significance. Figural Ottoman textiles are not wholly undocumented, but why on earth should *crocodiles* be offered? It would scarcely be worth mention but for the fact that Marino Sanuto[8] describes silks decorated with *cocodrili* worn officially in one of the great processions held on feast-days in Venice. The accounts given by Ibn Iyās, and doubtless Marino Sanuto too, are good evidence that the pattern was dependent upon the importance of a gift. It serves as a reminder that, though many gifts of textiles from the Ottomans to Italy, or vice versa, were to office-holders of the corresponding rank rather than to individual personalities, hence were fully hierarchical, the reverse view, or misconception, must have as frequently prevailed: materials must often, even mostly, have been presented to individuals on 'the other side' who nevertheless deserved well.

NOTES TO CHAPTER 7

1 If restrictions on the wearing of cloth of gold were so faithfully observed, however, it is hard to explain why in the 1570s the authorities suddenly became aware that there were 318 looms for cloth of gold in Istanbul alone, even if many or most of them were producing low-quality fabric. The large number argues for the absence of control on both the consumer and the production side.

2 Marino Sanuto, *Diarii* LVI (1900–1), 828.

3 Marino Sanuto, *Diarii* XLI (1894), 529.

4 Marino Sanuto, *Diarii* XXV (1889), 626–32.

5 L. A. Mayer, *Mamluk Costume* (Geneva 1952), 56–64.

6 M. Zarif Orgun, 'Osmanlı imperatorluğunda name ve hediye getiren elçilere yapılan merasim', *Türk Tarih Vesikaları* I/6 (1942), 407–13.

7 Gaston Wiet, *Journal d'un bourgeois du Caire. Chronique d'Ibn Iyâs* II (Paris 1960), 277. Ibn Iyās states that the robes were sent to Cairo in confirmation of his appointment. The 'crocodiles' were, however, a sign of distinction for, ten years previously (ibid., I/165) Şehzade Ḳorḳūd, the son of Bāyazīd II, was presented with a similar robe at the Cairo Citadel by the Mamlūk Sultan al-Ghawrī.

8 Marino Sanuto, *Diarii* XIII (1883), 130–4, describing the procession on 10 October 1511. The vestments worn by members of the Scuola di San Rocco included two of silver brocade, and two copes or capes (*cape*) *con do cocodrili dentro*. Had they been *dragons*, he would certainly have described them as such.

8

Wool and mohair

THE enormous export trade in raw silk from Bursa and raw cotton from Aleppo[1] in the sixteenth and seventeenth century to Europe was more than balanced by imports of fine woollen cloths to the Levant. Wool had traditionally been used for the garb of the higher *ʿulamā'*, who were consistently opposed to conspicuous consumption, even if their disapproval of silk and cloth of gold might not be sufficient to dissuade the authorities from using such fabrics. Fine woollens, which, however, could easily be as expensive as the finest silk brocades, were also much in demand at the Ottoman Court for heavy winter garments, and we must assume that the large quantities of Florentine woollens sold by Giovanni de Francesco Maringhi to the drapers of Galata[2] in the early sixteenth century were in fact for the Court, not for the *ʿulama'*, for these were essentially luxury fabrics, being first and foremost *scarlet* (the finest shorn woollen cloth, essentially crimson-dyed, though the 1505 Treasury inventory of Bāyazīd II also lists white and purple [*mor*] scarlets).[3] Such cloth was made all over Europe, often with Spanish merino wool, in Flanders, Brabant, Lombardy, Florence, Barcelona, England and France. By the later seventeenth century, English and French woollen exports to the Levant had virtually cornered the market and the only woollens listed even in the 1640 Istanbul register are Italian scarlets (*parangon*, from Italian *paragone*), patterned Florentine cloth, and dyed woollens, including some novelties (*turfanda*), from England (*londura*), Paris and Carcassonne in Languedoc.[4]

Some woollens were, of course, made within the Ottoman domains. Thrace, in particular Salonike, with its great Jewish merchant population, many of them Sephardic refugees from Spain, had always had a reputation for woollen cloth (*jūkh, çūḳā, çuha*), which was issued to the Janissaries for uniforms, among other things, as early as the reign of Bāyazīd II.[5] And when – as part of the Westernizing reforms of Selīm III (1789–1807) – the Ottoman army was issued with uniforms of European type, the enormous demand was expeditiously satisfied by the Jewish merchant drapers of Thrace and Bulgaria. One may guess that the cloth was mass-produced and rarely of high quality, for the only references to Thracian woollen fabrics in the Court inventories are to felts, which were as much used as carpets or heavily embroidered silks for floor coverings in the Palace.

In conspicuous contrast to this dependence of the Ottoman Empire for fine woollens upon Northern and Western Europe was its exploitation of the mohair industry. Mohair cloths, known to Europe from the time of Marco Polo onwards[6] as camlets (Italian, *ciambellotti*), evidently from the popular belief that they were made from or contained camel hair, were in great demand. The accounts of Giovanni de Francesco Maringhi, for example, show that although he was largely engaged in financing purchases of raw silk at Bursa through the sale of Florentine woollens in Galata, only buying pieces of woven Bursa silks in response to specific Florentine orders, there was a constant demand in Europe, and indeed in Istanbul among the colonies of resident foreigners, for mohair cloths.

The Angora goat may have been introduced to the Anatolian plateau as early as the reign of the Byzantine Emperor Justinian (527–565). The peculiar fineness of its fleece was highly appreciated as the description, recorded in the late seventeenth century by the French botanist, Tournefort, shows:[7]

> They breed the finest goats in the world in the Champaign of *Angora*. They are of a dazzling white; and their Hair, which is fine as Silk, naturally curl'd in Locks of eight or nine inches long, is work'd up into the finest stuffs, specially Camlet: but they don't suffer these Fleeces to be exported unspun, because the Country People gain their Livelihood thereby. *Strabo* seems to have spoken of these fine Goats: In the *Neighbourhood of the River Halys*, says he, *they breed Sheep, whose Wool is very thick and soft; and besides, there are Goats, not to be met with anywhere else*. However it be, these fine Goats are to be seen only within four or five days Journey of *Angora* and *Beibazar*; their Young are degenerate if they are

carried farther. The Thred made of this Goat's Hair is sold from four Livres to twelve or fifteen Livres the Oque; there is some sold even for twenty or five and twenty Crowns the Oque; but this is only made up into Camlet for the Use of the Grand Signior's Seraglio. The Workmen of *Angora* use this Thred of Goat's Hair without mixture, whereas at *Brussels* they are oblig'd to mix Thred made of Wool, for what reason I know not. In *England* they mix up this Hair in their Perriwigs, but it must not be spun. In this consists the Riches of *Angora*; all the Inhabitants are employ'd in this Trade.

Other Western travellers expressed surprise that the Venetians, who were by far the largest purchasers of mohair cloths, had never domesticated the Angora goat on the Venetian Terraferma: they may have tried and found that the goats did not thrive; or perhaps they prudently decided that they preferred the Terraferma as it was, rich and productive, rather than deforested and eroded like the central Anatolian steppe. Records for the sixteenth century in the archives of the kadis' court at Ankara show that foreigners were actually engaged in making large purchases of Angora wool, but the highly protectionist attitude of the Ottoman authorities which Tournefort notes was very probably for fiscal reasons, since taxes were levied at all stages of the manufacture of mohair wool and cloth and went to the current owner of the mohair tax farm. These dues could be very onerous, as is shown by an edict dated 14 Rabīʿ I 998/23 January 1590[8] from the Court in Istanbul stating that Venetian merchants who had been exempted by treaty from taxes imposed on mohair at Ankara were nevertheless being charged for a whole variety of dues and that this practice must stop.

Ottoman protectionism was not, however, entirely fiscally motivated. In the seventeenth century there are several records of temporary embargoes put upon the export of mohair cloths from Ankara, suggesting that the Ottoman authorities were well aware of the usefulness of such bans as a political weapon against Western Europe.[9]

The earliest, as well as one of the most graphic, descriptions of the manufacture of mohair cloth occurs in the Letters of Ogier Ghiselin de Busbecq, who in the 1550s was the ambassador of the Holy Roman Emperor Charles V to the Sublime Porte:[10]

> Here [Ankara] we also saw how the watered camlet [mohair] . . . made from the hair of goats, is dyed or given by means of a press its watered appearance from the 'waves' produced by pouring water upon it. The pieces which have received the marks of very broad 'waves' in continuous lines are considered the best and choicest. If the 'waves' are smaller and of varying lengths and run into one another, though the colour and material may be the same, this is counted as a defect, and the cloth is valued at a price less by several gold pieces. The wearing of this cloth is a mark of distinction among the older Turks of high rank. Soleiman himself does not like to be seen wearing any material but this, and prefers a green colour, which, though to our eyes unsuited to a man of advanced years, is commended by their religion and the practice of Mahomet, their prophet, who even in old age habitually wore it.
>
> Black is considered a mean and unfortunate colour, and for anyone to appear in black unlucky and ill-omened; so much so, that on several occasions the Pashas expressed their astonishment, and even seriously complained, because we approached them clad in black. No-one in Turkey ever appears publicly in black raiment, unless he is the victim of serious financial loss or some other heavy calamity. Purple [crimson] is held to confer distinction, but is regarded in time of war as prophetic of death; white, yellow, blue, violet and mouse-colour are considered luckier.

The precise economic or industrial reasons for the concentration of the mohair industry upon Ankara are unclear. The 1640 Istanbul price register also lists patterned mohair from Tosya (south of Kastamonu) and Koçhisar in Central Anatolia; though at much lower prices than for Ankara cloths. The simplest reason is probably the right one: the skill of the Ankara weavers was superior, so that the close Ottoman fiscal regulation was in fact fully rational. But, by the early sixteenth century even, Ankara was thronged with foreigners – Italians, French, Russians, Poles, Catalans, and, later Dutch and English merchants, all of them prepared to agree to the hardest bargains the Ottoman authorities could strike.[11]

In addition to the imported heavy woollen luxury cloths and Ankara mohair, the Ottomans also used *shawls* in various ways. These were woven at Bursa and Gürün, but from an early date were also imported from Lahore and from Kashmir in the Indian sub-continent, as well as from central and eastern Iran and from North Africa. They were mostly produced wholesale, in standard lengths and widths. Lahore shawls were known as Müreccah (Superior), ʿAnbarsar (Amber-headed) and Valide (the Queen Mother's), some of them being striped. The Valide patterns were dense, the most popular being the one that became known later as the Paisley bud pattern, with coiled pear-shaped *boteh* motifs.

At both Bursa and Ankara were manufactured silk materials called *Şalākī* copying these shawl designs. Antoine Galland, in his journal of his stay in Istanbul

(1671–2), states that in winter the Turks cover their feet and legs with wraps called *chales* made of hare's fur. But in fact shawls were much more widely used: the 1680 Palace inventory lists Kashmiri and Chios shawls of all sorts and patterns. Mouradjea d'Ohsson, who was much struck by their fineness (a shawl measuring 3·70 × 1·25 m would easily pass through a ring), stated that they were worn as sashes by both sexes. As for the winter, shawls were worn by men, whether mounted or on foot, against the weather, for the Turks, he says, do not carry umbrellas and only women travel by carriage.[12]

Notes to Chapter 8

1 E. Ashtor, 'Les lainages dans l'Orient médiéval' in *Atti della seconda settimana di studi, Istituto F. Datini* (Florence 1976), 657–86; Ugo Tucci, 'Un ciclo di affari in Siria (1579–81)' in U. Tucci, *Mercanti, Navi, Monete nel Cinquecento Veneto* (Bologna 1981), 95–143; Ralph Davis, *Aleppo and Devonshire Square* (London 1967); B. Dini, 'Aspetti del commercio de esportazione dei panni di lana e dei drappi di seta fiorentina in Costantinopoli, negli anni 1522–1531' in *Studi in memoria di Federigo Melis* (Naples 1975) IV, 1–54.

2 G. R. B. Richards, *Florentine Merchants in the Age of the Medici* (Cambridge, Mass. 1932).

3 J. H. Munro, 'The Medieval Scarlet and the economics of sartorial splendour' in *Cloth and Clothing in Medieval Europe. Essays in Memory of Professor E. M. Carus-Wilson*, ed. N. B. Harte and K. G. Pontin (London 1983), 13–70. Munro argues that white and purple scarlets were either undyed woollens or woollens which had not undergone the full processing to turn them into crimsons. The fiery scarlet colour which is now typical of the cloth is the result of using a chrome mordant, a practice which does not predate the seventeenth century in Europe and which may well have been introduced much later in Ottoman Turkey.

4 M. S. Kütükoğlu, *Osmanlılarda narh müessesesi ve 1640 tarihli narh defteri* (Istanbul 1983), 109–10.

5 H. Sahillioğlu, 'Yeniçeri çuhası ve II. Bayazid'in son yıllarında Yeniçeri çuha muhasebesi', *Güney-Doğu Avrupa Araştırmaları Dergisi* 2–3 (1973–4), 415–67. The best general study of the Thracian wool industry is by Benjamin Braude, 'International competition and domestic cloth in the Ottoman Empire in 1500–1650: A study in undevelopment', *Review* (Fernand Braudel Centre) II/3 (1979), 437–51.

6 P. Pelliot, *Notes on Marco Polo* I (Paris 1959), No. 109, s.v. 'Camlet'.

7 *A Voyage into the Levant, by M. Tournefort*, trans. Anon. (London 1741), 300–1.

8 Halit Ongan, *Ankara'nın iki numeralı şer'iye sicilleri* (Ankara 1974), No. 1692.

9 Suraiya Faroqhi, 'Onyedinci yüzyıl Ankara'sında sof imalatı ve sof atölyeleri', *Istanbul Üniversitesi Iktisat Fakültesi Mecmuası* 41/1–4, 1982–3 (Istanbul 1984), 237–59.

10 *The Turkish Letters of Ogier Ghiselin de Busbecq, Imperial Ambassador at Constantinople 1554–1562*, Translated from the Latin of the Elzevir edition of 1633 by Edward Seymour Forster (Oxford 1927; 1968), 50.

11 Suraiya Faroqhi, 'Textile production in Rumeli and the Arab provinces: Geographical distribution and internal trade (1560–1650)', *Osmanlı Araştırmaları/The Journal of Ottoman Studies* I (Istanbul 1980), 61–83; ead., *Towns and Townsmen of Ottoman Anatolia. Trade, crafts and food production in an urban setting, 1520–1650* (Cambridge 1984), 125–55.

12 D'Ohsson, *Tableau Général de l'Empire Ottoman* IV (Paris 1891), 132–4.

9

The Ottoman fur trade

LIKE the Mamlūk Sultans in Egypt, the Ottoman State was a great consumer of furs, to line or trim robes of honour for distribution, and the kaftans for the Sultans' own wardrobes as well. Furs had been a natural concomitant of the trade in slaves to man the Mamlūk armies, since both were sold essentially in the same Crimean markets.[1] These fell to the Ottomans with the capture of Kaffa in 1475 by Meḥmed II: the slave trade to the Mamlūk State seems to have continued up to the conquest of Egypt by Selīm I in 1516–17, but the furs increasingly were diverted to the Ottoman capital.

The uninterrupted victories and conquests of the Ottomans in the first half of the sixteenth century, when bales of furs – like those from the Safavid palace, the Heşt Bihişt at Tabriz, which was sacked shortly after Selīm I's victory at Çaldıran in 1514 – appear regularly in lists of booty, must have made State control of the fur trade largely superfluous, even though the demand for furs to adorn robes of honour was steadily increasing. It seems highly probably, however, that in the following decades, as the supply of furs, rich textiles, porcelains and plate from these victorious campaigns dried up, the Palace took the matter in hand and commissioned merchants to guarantee the supply of furs. For this the Ottomans seem to have adopted the Mamlūk system, of State merchants, specially appointed to supply not just slaves for the army, but strategic materials such as timber and iron or steel. Interestingly, moreover, by the later sixteenth century, when official records more regularly mention these State merchants (*Ḫāṣṣa tuccār-ları*), they are trading not with the Crimea or with Poland but specifically with Muscovy, where international trade was highly bureaucratized.

Recourse to Muscovy, which increasingly was appearing as the Northern enemy of the Ottoman empire, may not have been a matter of choice. For, because of over-trapping, there was in the sixteenth century a marked contraction in the supply of furs, which led fur-merchants to travel further and further afield in their search for fine pelts. Simultaneously, however, the trappers in Muscovy were moving steadily eastwards towards the Urals and Siberia.[2] This led to the diversion of the export trade to the Volga-Caspian route leading not to Istanbul but to Safavid Iran, which, until well into the seventeenth century, was the Ottomans' sworn enemy. The eastwards deflection simultaneously lessened the capacity of Russian and Polish fur-traders to satisfy the growing demand in Western Europe, so that the Ottomans were faced with serious competition simultaneously on two fronts. Hence the importance of State merchants, to collar as much of the trade as they could, to cut out foreign competition and to keep the major profits of the fur trade within the control of the Ottoman State. The probability that the Sultans wished to create a State monopoly is thus quite high.[3]

The only detailed study of the Ottoman fur trade to date covers the period 1558–87,[4] a period when strong Tsars gave Muscovy the internal security to guarantee long-distance trade on a large scale: in the time of troubles in the early seventeenth century following the death of Boris Godunov, for example, the fur trade was again seriously disrupted. The Muscovite regulations were strict: only properly accredited foreign merchants, or those with some diplomatic status, were allowed direct access to Moscow; the remainder were allowed no nearer than Putivl', some 500 km south-west of Moscow. Secondly, certain commodities, notably gold and silver, arms, sables and probably other furs too, fish-tooth and amber, as well as wax and Russian or Bolghary leather, were monopolies reserved to the Tsars. Their export was controlled by State merchants from the Moscow Treasury who fixed the prices unilaterally and often, foreigners complained, extortionately.[5]

The complications of the Muscovite system and the scarcity of furs made the appointment of Ottoman counterparts to them with the requisite official status a virtual essential. Too little is yet known, however, to say whether the state merchants were a corps, to which fur-merchants would then have been conscripted or co-opted, or whether appointments were occasional or limited to a particular journey. But they were, anyway, financed by the Ottoman Treasury with large amounts of cash – 500,000 akçe (1529); 600,000 akçe (1542).[6] If furs were an essential to the Ottoman honours system, however, they were a vast expense; the supply was difficult to maintain and, worst of all, Muscovy was generally unwilling to purchase Ottoman goods in large enough quantity to balance the drain in cash to the Ottoman Treasury. By great good fortune, however, in the later sixteenth century there grew up a Russian demand for the Bursa silks (cf. p. 33), which could then be used to finance the purchase of furs.[7] Those purchased in this way were, as a matter of treaty obligation or customary usage (it is not clear which), to be exempt from customs duties inside Muscovy, in the Ottoman tributary states and inside the Ottoman domains. From the reign of Bāyazīd II right up to the fixed-price register of 1050/1640–1 (cf. p. 162) there are records of rich furs being sold on the open market in Istanbul. The State merchants therefore must have used their official status to obtain furs, or other goods, on their own account. Even if the Ottoman Court could not enforce monopolistic control, however, its means, its priority of choice and possibly even the special terms it received gave it privileged access to the fur trade.

Ottoman demand for furs was, of course, substantially similar to that in Mamlūk Egypt, in Safavid Iran and in contemporary Europe.[8] The only surprising thing is that so little is known of how the trade worked in detail. There is no parallel to Ibn Baṭṭūṭa's famous description in the 1330s of the story he had heard of the Land of Darkness, forty days' journey beyond the town of Bolghary on the Volga in the trans-Ural steppe.[9] It was a form of 'spirit market' or dumb trade in which Muslim merchants obtained the furs they wanted by barter without ever seeing the trappers. They would appear during the night and leave their wares on the ground; the merchants would take what they wanted, leaving goods in payment for what they took; and the trappers would remove the rest, and the goods in payment, as soon as they had departed.

The range of skins was also substantially similar to those available in late medieval and Renaissance Europe (apart from lion-, leopard- and tiger-skins, which are mentioned in the 1505 inventory of the Treasury of Bāyazīd II), though without the cheap varieties (cat, rabbit and rat) which were in common European use. They were mostly marten, fox, squirrel (vair),[10] ermine, beaver, lynx and sable. There were, however, differences in taste: in Europe in the sixteenth and seventeenth centuries there was a great vogue for marten, whereas, for most of the time, in Ottoman Turkey the most highly esteemed was sable. Under the mentally unbalanced Sultan Ibrāhīm (1640–8), whose excessive craving for sables, even for furnishings to strew about the Palace apartments, led him to promulgate levies of sable pelts from the various classes of Ottoman society, the supply was far from sufficient to cater for the demand and as a result prices rose drastically on the Istanbul market.

The skins came as *timbres*,[11] a standard quantity, varying with the type of fur in question, of skins packed between two boards. The pelts were then sized and graded and priced accordingly. In the 1640–1 price list for the Istanbul markets,[12] just before the inflation caused by Sultan Ibrāhīm's passion, the most expensive were extra-large sable heads or paws (12,000 and 11,000 akçe respectively), smaller sizes being correspondingly cheaper, and then, in steadily descending order, Circassian marten (whole skins, throat fur and paws), Thracian polecat (*sansar*), ermine, squirrel, white fox, Bosnian and Anatolian wolf, jackal fur from the Dardanelles and from Karaman, and, finally, fox paws. This is a wider selection than inventories associated with the Palace give, but the market obviously had to cater not only for the rich who simply wanted conspicuous luxury trimmings or linings, but also for people less well off who simply needed some protection against the vicious cold of an Istanbul winter and who would therefore be satisfied with something coarser and locally obtained, rather than a prestige import.

The prices in the 1640–1 register give very little indication that quality, which must have been extremely variable, was a factor in determining the proper price. Official regulations were in general content to specify the maximum number of pelts to be used in lining kaftans for presentation, as in the Bursa market regulations for 1502, or to complain that the furriers were cheating by using fewer pelts than their predecessors had used. An edict dated late Şaʿbān 1106/late April 1695,[13] for example, orders the furriers of Istanbul and Edirne to return to former practice and use, for one complete fur lining, 80 sable, 70 lynx belly, 150 ermine, 90 sable paws, 200 squirrel, and so on. It also prohibits the re-use of old sables from made-up furs. In official eyes quantity appears to have been more important than quality. The matching and display of pelts to the best effect was, of course, a matter of the greatest skill, hence the subject of regulations in the statutes of the furriers' guilds in medieval and Renaissance Europe:[14] but the Ottoman authorities may have taken for granted that the use of inferior skins would invariably show up. The linings of some of the kaftans in the Topkapı collections show that work of the highest quality was available to the Palace. Not content with this, indeed, Ottoman furriers sewed patterns of dyed furs or furs from different animals to set each other off. Interestingly, furs were only used for linings: the modern fur coat would seem a pointless anachronism in Ottoman Turkey. The heavy gowns they made up were not only for Sultans but also for their viziers (*erkân kürküsü*).

Mouradjea d'Ohsson's *Tableau Général de l'Empire Ottoman* describes how in the eighteenth century the wearing of furs at the Ottoman Court had ultimately become a ritual. The preference of Selīm III (1789–1807) was for black fox, which was therefore held to be the most precious fur and its use consequently forbidden to anyone else. When viziers were invested, they were presented with fur-lined robes, and Court officials wore their furs at the Sultan's command. When autumn came, d'Ohsson says,[15] they put on ermine, three weeks later squirrel and then sables for the rest of the winter. However, when the Sultan changed his furs, the officials had to change theirs too.

By the seventeenth century there had developed a numerous corporation of furriers in Istanbul and Edirne, headed by a Chief Furrier (Kürkçübaşı), an official with responsibilities to the Court, who was often extremely rich. For example, Süleymān the Magnificent's Chief Furrier, Aḥmed Beg, endowed mosques at Cerrahpaşa and at Istinye on the Bosphorus, and another Chief Furrier, Ḥüseyin Ağa, built a mosque at Yedikule in 1022/1613–14. The workshops were largely concentrated in the Kürkçü Han (the furriers' caravansaray or depot), which was certainly in existence by the mid-seventeenth century, since there is a contemporary report that it was damaged in 1652 by one of the fires which periodically swept the bazar quarters of Istanbul. There were almost certainly other workshops across the Golden Horn in Galata, however, catering to the European colony or executing work for orders from Europe. We do not know where the orders for the Palace were executed, but the concentration of the workshops and the appointment of a Court official to head the furriers' guild suggests that they were executed by the furriers in the Kürkçü Han.

Notes to Chapter 9

1 Pero Tafur, *Andanças e viajes de un hidalgo español (1436–9)*, ed. J. Vives in *Gesammelte Aufsätze zur Kulturgeschichte Spaniens, Spanische Forschungen der Görresgesellschaft* VII (Münster 1938), 162–3.

2 S. V. Kirikov, *Izmeneniya zhivotnogo mira v prirodnykh zonakh SSSR (XIII–XIX vv.), stepnaya zona i lesostep'* (Moscow 1960), *passim*. For the routes see V. E. Syroyechkovsky, 'Puti i usloviya snoshenii Moskvy s Krymom na rubezhe XVI veka', *Izvestiya Akademii Nauk SSSR, Otdeleniye Obshchestvennykh Nauk* VII/3 (1932), 193–237.

3 There is an edict, dated mid-Cumādā II 1168/early April 1755, controlling the furriers in Istanbul, but it is more specifically concerned with regulating workshops (by the particular sort of fur they worked) and specifying the quantities allowable for summer- and winter-weight garments than with regulating sale or distribution. Cf. Ahmet Refik, *Hicrî on ikinci asırda Istanbul hayatı (1100–1200)* (Istanbul 1930), No. 218. It is unclear to what extent this edict was repeating earlier decrees or how far it was an extempore response to some new or sudden shortage.

4 A. Bennigsen and Ch. Lemercier-Quelquejay, 'Les marchands de la cour ottomane et le commerce des fourrures moscovites dans la seconde moitié du XVIe siècle', *Cahiers du Monde Russe et Slave* XI/3 (1970), 363–90. Cf. also Benjamin Braude, 'Venture and faith in the commercial life of the Ottoman Balkans, 1500–1650', *The International History Review* VII (Simon Fraser University, Burnaby, B.C. 1985), 519–42: I am indebted to the author for this citation.

5 Giles Fletcher, *Of the Ruse Commonwealth*, in *Russia at the close of the 16th century*, ed. E. A. Bond (Hakluyt Society, London 1856), 57. Cf. J. L. B. Martin, *Treasure of the Land of Darkness. The Fur Trade and its Significance for Medieval Russia* (Cambridge 1986).

6 M. Fekhner, *Torgovlya Russkogo gosudarstva so stranami Vostoka v XVI v.*, 2nd ed. (Moscow 1956), 85.

7 F. Dalsar, *Türk sanayi ve ticaret tarihinde Bursa'da ipekçilik* (Istanbul 1960), 192–4, cites, for example, an edict dated 15 Rabīʿ I 992/27 March 1584, appointing merchants to buy tin, Russian leather and sables in Muscovy, to be financed with Bursa silks in lieu of cash from the Sultan's Treasury. There are sporadic records of Russians at Bursa from the late fifteenth century or early sixteenth century onwards; cf. H. Inalcık, 'Bursa and the commerce of the Levant', *Journal of the Economic and Social History of the Orient* III (1960), 131–47. They were certainly there for the trade, but what their official status was and what they were there to buy – raw silk or woven silks – is mostly not clear.

8 L. A. Mayer, *Mamluk Costume* (Geneva 1952), 56–64; Robert Delort, *Le commerce des fourrures en Occident à la fin du moyen age (vers 1300–vers 1450)* (Rome 1978).

9 *The Travels of Ibn Baṭṭūṭa*, translated and revised H. A. R. Gibb, II (Hakluyt Society, Cambridge 1962), 491–2. Gibb remarks that there is a virtually identical account of this dumb trade in Abu'l-Fidā, *Taqwīm al-Buldān*, ed. J. Reinaud (Paris 1840) I, 284, that author's geographical survey being virtually contemporary with Ibn Baṭṭūṭa's.

10 P. Pelliot, *Notes on Marco Polo* (Paris 1963), No. 219, 'Ercolin'.

11 *Early voyages and travel to Russia and Persia*, ed. E. D. Morgan (Hakluyt Society, London 1886), 207, note 2. Paolo Giovio adds that the finest sables, fox and lynx (*loups-cerviers*) came packed in this way from Perm' and Pechora beyond the Urals; cf. *Sigismund von Herberstein, Rerum Moscovitarum Commentarii*, ed. R. H. Major, (Hakluyt Society, London 1852), 242–3.

12 M. S. Kütükoğlu, *Osmanlılarda narh müessesesi ve 1640 tarihli narh defteri* (Istanbul 1983), 165–8. The price the furriers may charge for 'poor man's furs' is also stipulated.

13 Ahmet Refik, *Hicrî on ikinci asırda Istanbul hayatı (1100–1200)* (Istanbul 1930), No. 29.

14 The statutes of the furriers (Mandement de la Vairie) of Paris in 1433 – cited in V. Gay, *Glossaire archéologique du Moyen Age et de la Renaissance* I (Paris 1887), 740, s.v. 'Fourreur' – strictly specify the number of skins, and also prescribe, for example, that back, belly and side fur should not be mixed but each made up separately.

15 D'Ohsson, *Tableau Général de l'Empire Ottoman* IV (Paris 1791), 134–8.

CAPTIONS AND NOTES TO ILLUSTRATIONS
1–85

Attributions and dating

The grounds for the attributions are for the most part not stated by the standard authorities on the Costumes in the Topkapı Saray. Some garments bear labels, which may be more or less acceptable; some are from Royal tombs; some are similar to fabrics depicted in portraits of individual Sultans; and some may be attributed on grounds of general plausibility to a particular ruler. As for the dating, the presumption is that fabrics tailored for the Sultans would generally have been recent, as well as brand new. Some fabrics are broadly datable by internal criteria (design, technique, etc.); yet others may have been dated by reference to the personages to whom they have been ascribed. Since there is scope for error, both in the attributions and the dating, I have generally preferred to use the expression 'associated with', which avoids the often tricky problem of whether they were woven or made up for that particular individual. The dating is within a very wide tolerance and, I hope, correct even if the attributions noted in the captions are challenged or rejected.

Bibliographical citations

Works cited frequently in the notes on the illustrations are given in abbreviated form; for complete bibliographical details in such cases see p. 211.

1 Short-sleeved kaftan, somewhat implausibly associated with Meḥmed II, the Conqueror (1451–81), crimson velvet with brocading in gold and silver thread, with alternating stars and rosettes of fat tulip buds and stylized pomegranates separated by tiger-stripes, lined partially with yellow satin; 13/8. Length 142·5 cm.
It is difficult to believe the design is as old as the mid-fifteenth century; it looks a good century later.

2 Short-sleeved kaftan, possibly to be associated with Meḥmed II, the Conqueror (1451–81), silk velvet with crimson tiger-stripes and leopard-spots on a golden ground, with lining partially of stamped green satin; 13/6. Length 117 cm.
□ Cf. L. Mackie in E. Atıl (ed.), *Turkish Art*, No. 205, who more reasonably attributes it to Istanbul or Bursa, sixteenth century.

3 Short-sleeved, fur-lined kaftan, associated with Bāyazīd II (1481–1512), brocaded crimson velvet with heavy looping stems of serrated leaves filled with polychrome blossoms on a ground of lighter floral scrolls in voided velvet, sixteenth century; 13/35. Length 141 cm.
□ Tahsin Öz, *Turkish Textiles and Velvets*, xix and Plate XVIII.

4 Long-sleeved fawn satin kaftan with quilted lining, associated with Bāyazīd II (1481–1512), *c.* 1500; 13/34. Length 92 cm (very short!).

5 Short-sleeved heavy ivory satin kaftan, associated with Selīm I, the Grim (1512–20), sixteenth century, with quilted cotton lining; 13/40. Length 144 cm.

6 Short-sleeved short kaftan, associated with Bāyazīd II (1481–1512), multi coloured silk brocaded satin (*serenk*), basically crimson with the design principally in golden silk of highly stylized lotuses or tulips and bud motifs with a filling of blossoms or scales, sixteenth century; 13/38. Length 87 cm.
The attribution is somewhat questionable.
□ Tahsin Öz, *Turkish Textiles and Velvets*, Plate X (with an attribution to Bāyazīd II); *The Anatolian Civilisations*, E 136.

7 (and detail) Short-sleeved kaftan with quilted cotton lining, bearing a label stating that it belonged to Selīm I, the Grim (1512–20), crimson rucked brocaded satin, with a design of pointed hastate motifs with light foliate and floral trails, sixteenth century; 13/46. Length 138·5 cm.
□ Tahsin Öz, *Turkish Textiles and Velvets*, Plate XXIV; L. Mackie in E. Atıl (ed.), *Turkish Art*, No. 201 ('mid-16th century, Istanbul or Bursa'); *The Anatolian Civilisations*, E 102.

8 (and detail) Short-sleeved kaftan, associated with Selīm I, the Grim (1512–20), of quilted silk brocaded satin (*serenk*), diagonally ridged, with triple-spot motifs in hastate foliate medallions in tones of yellow and black, lined partially with crimson silk, sixteenth century; 13/42. Length 140·5 cm.
□ Tahsin Öz, *Turkish Textiles and Velvets*, Plate XXIII.

9 Long-sleeved ceremonial kaftan, associated with Selīm I, the Grim (1512–20), of fine lamé or cloth of gold, with self designs of fat curling stems and stylized lotus medallions, possibly Italian, sixteenth century; 13/831. Length 158·5 cm.
To judge by the lengths of other garments associated with Selīm I (*ills. 5, 7, 8, 10*), which all have fairly standard measurements, this kaftan probably belonged to someone else.

10 Short-sleeved quilted kaftan with low collar, associated with Selīm I, the Grim (1512–20), of crimson brocaded satin (*serenk*), with triple-spot motif in golden silk outlined in blue, sixteenth century; 13/41. Length 144 cm.
□ Tahsin Öz, *Turkish Textiles and Velvets*, Plate XXII.

11 Short kaftan, associated with Selīm I, the Grim (1512–20), of crimson velvet lined partially with stamped golden satin, possibly early sixteenth century; 13/39. Length 87 cm.

12 Short-sleeved over-garment, associated with Selīm I, the Grim (1512–20), of watered leaf-green silk, lined partially with deep-blue stamped satin, sixteenth century; 13/830. Length 83·5 cm.
The length suggests that the kaftan was made for a youth.

13 Long-sleeved kaftan, associated with Süleymān the Magnificent (1520–66), of olive-green watered silk, lined with deep-blue and golden satin, sixteenth century; 13/110. Length 120 cm (very short).

14 Long-sleeved ceremonial kaftan associated with Süleymān the Magnificent (1520–66), cloth of gold or lamé (*serāser*) with voided velvet crimson tulips and feathery leaves in relief, sixteenth century; 13/840. Length 154·5 cm.
The fabric is most probably an Italian imitation, at some distance, from a Bursa medallion silk. The lining is partially of stamped golden-yellow satin.

15 Plain white satin kaftan of Süleymān the Magnificent (1520–66), with impressed medallions of triple spots, probably dating from the later years of his reign (when he is known to have favoured sober colours), after 1550; 13/99. Length 150 cm.

16 Short-sleeved greenish-yellow rucked satin kaftan with quilted cotton lining, associated with Süleymān the Magnificent (1520–66), *c.* 1550; 13/112. Length 150 cm.

17 Quilted short-sleeved kaftan of Süleymān the Magnificent (1520–66), ivory satin, lined partially with pale-green silk, sixteenth century; 13/111. Length 150 cm.

18 (and detail) Long-sleeved ceremonial kaftan, sometimes associated with Bāyazīd II (1481–1512) but more plausibly to be associated with one or other of Süleymān the Magnificent's sons, Şehzāde Bāyazīd (strangled 1561) or Muṣṭafā (d. 1553); 13/37. Length 150·5 cm.
The silk is a brocade with some gold and with brilliantly coloured trails of feathery leaves, floral sprays and stylized composite pomegranates, lotuses and rosettes on a dark ground, the design being so grandly conceived that the fabric shows no repeat. Other silks, equally brilliantly coloured but in a completely different colour-scheme on a ivory ground, were woven from the same pattern. One of these bears a label attributing it, implausibly, to Muṣṭafā II (1695–1703), and there may be a confusion of names here. Comparable treatment of the leaves is to be seen on some of the panels of tiles in the narthex of the mosque of Rüstem Paşa in Istanbul (inaugurated 1561) and on tile panels, probably of the same decade, facing the exterior of the Sünnet Odası in the Topkapı Saray. There are also parallels in Ottoman Court carpets woven in Cairo in the later sixteenth century. These may conceivably all be the work of the same designer in the Palace, but if so none of the other silks of the sixteenth and seventeenth centuries were.
□ *The Anatolian Civilisations* E 103; L. Mackie in E. Atıl (ed.), *Turkish Art*, Pl. 60.

19 (and detail) Short-sleeved kaftan, associated with Selīm II (1566–74), silver-brocaded silk, the silver wrapped on a yellow silk core, with a dense all-over pattern of undulating Prunus branches in flower, with a deep-crimson silk lining, sixteenth century; 13/176. Length 150 cm.

20 Short-sleeved kaftan, associated with Selīm II (1566–74), ivory silk with metal thread over a yellow silk core, with a design of large sunburst medallions with crescents containing smaller sunbursts and a rosette inside, tailored so that the design is absolutely central when the kaftan is fastened, later sixteenth century; 13/177. Length 137 cm.
□ L. Mackie in E. Atıl (ed.), *Turkish Art*, Plate 63 (with the attribution 'Istanbul, 16th century').

continued on page 153

Opposite
Ceremonial kaftan, seventeenth century;
see illustration 22

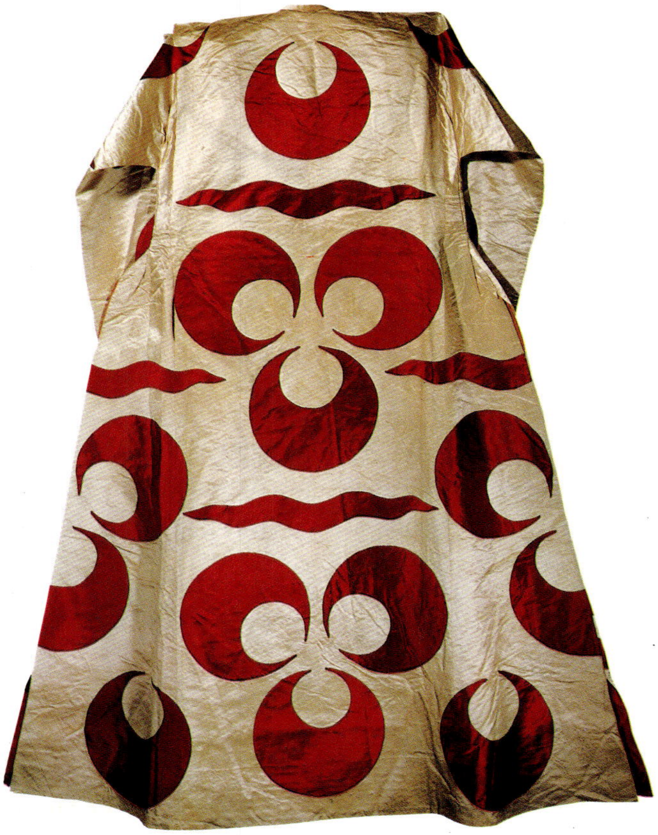

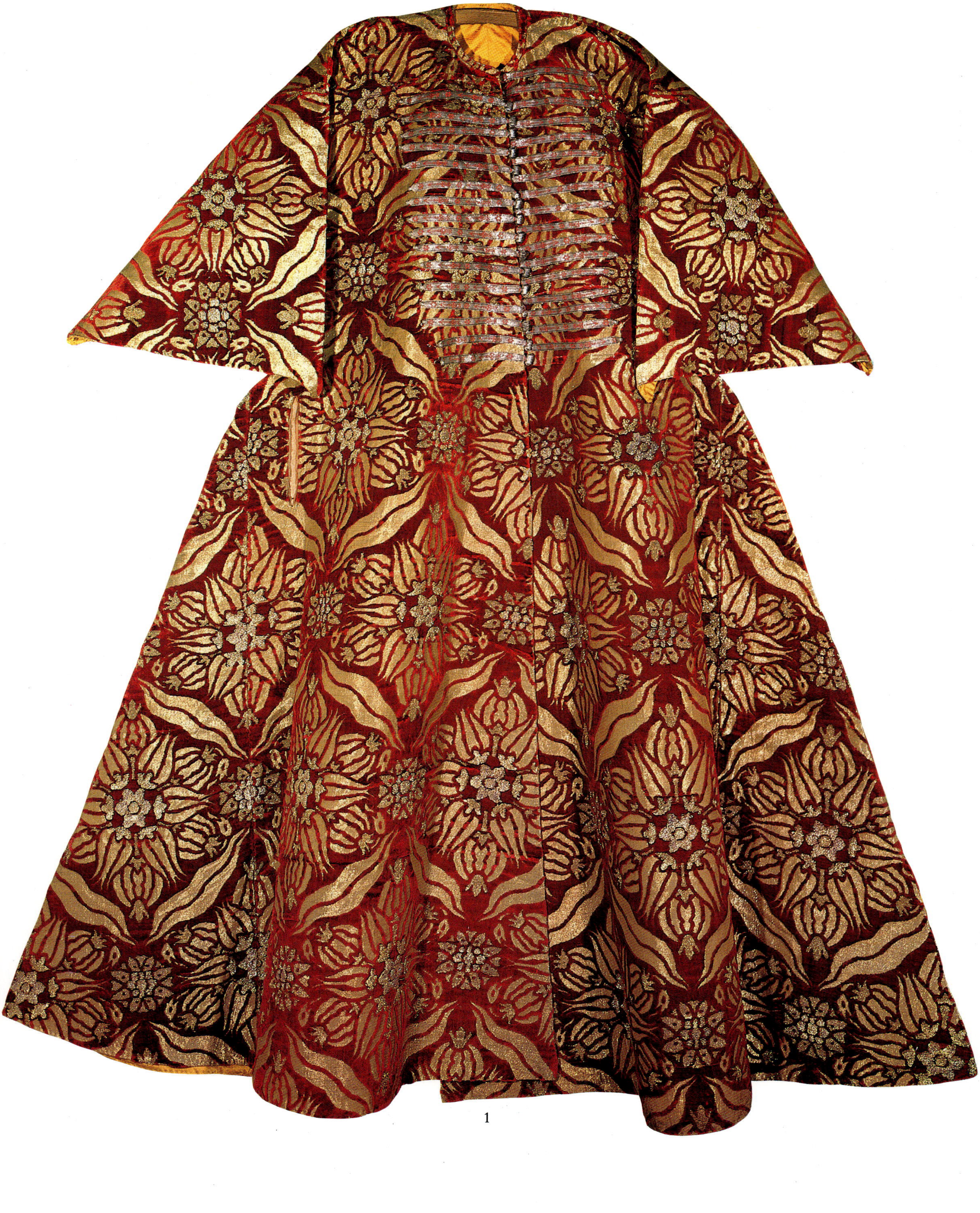

1

4

5

6

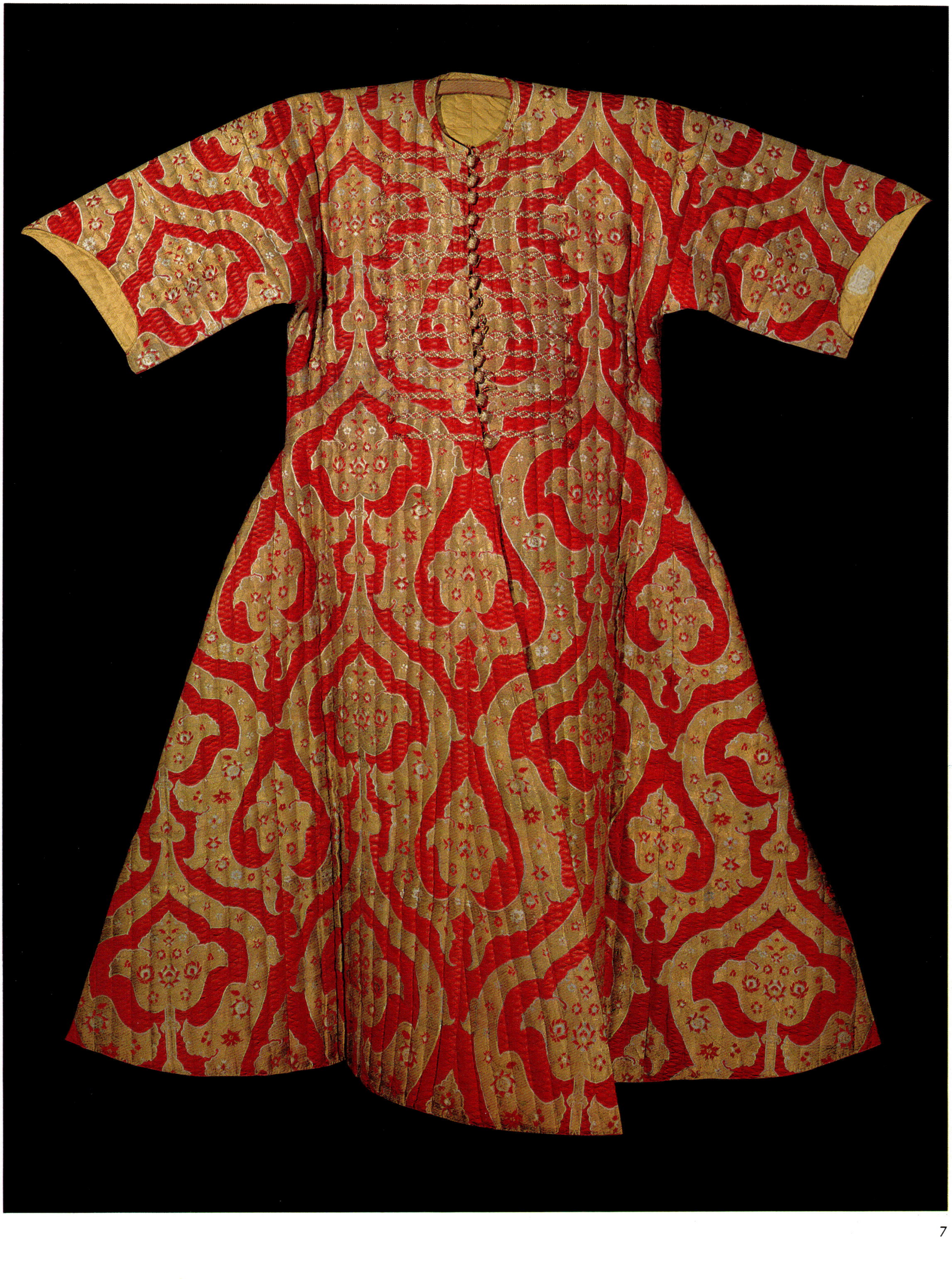

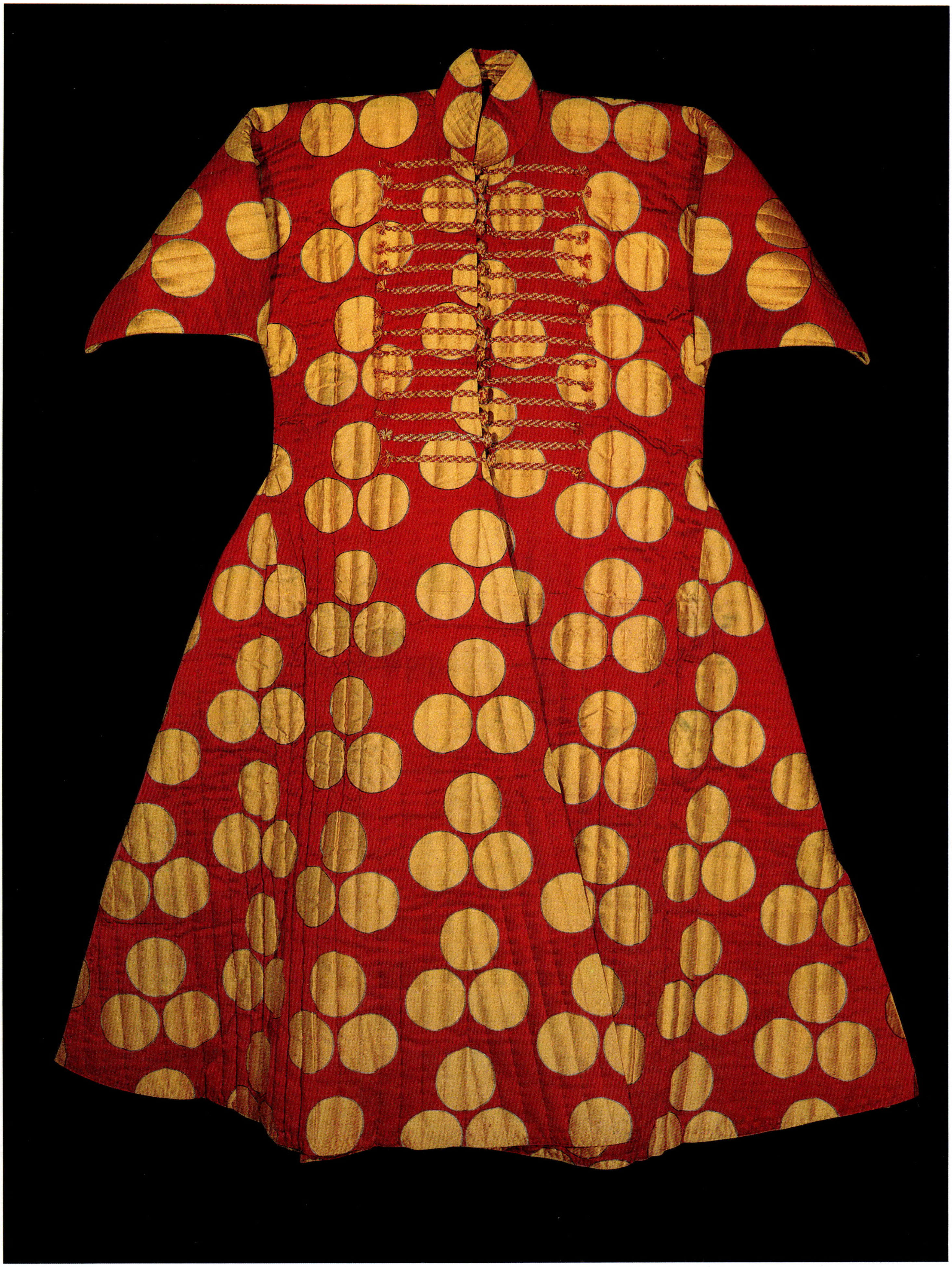

12

15

16

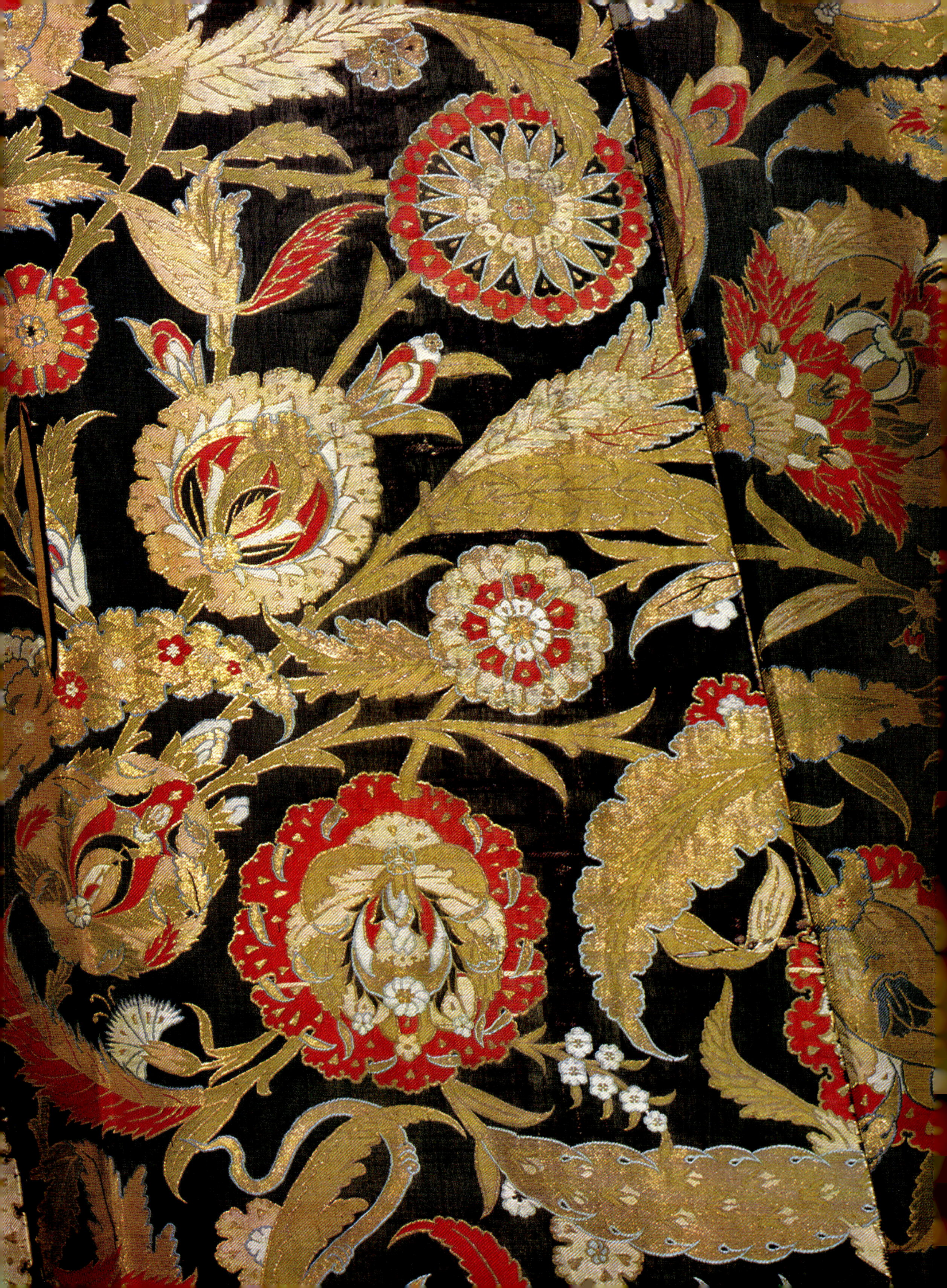

21

22

23

24

32

34

35

36

38

40

41

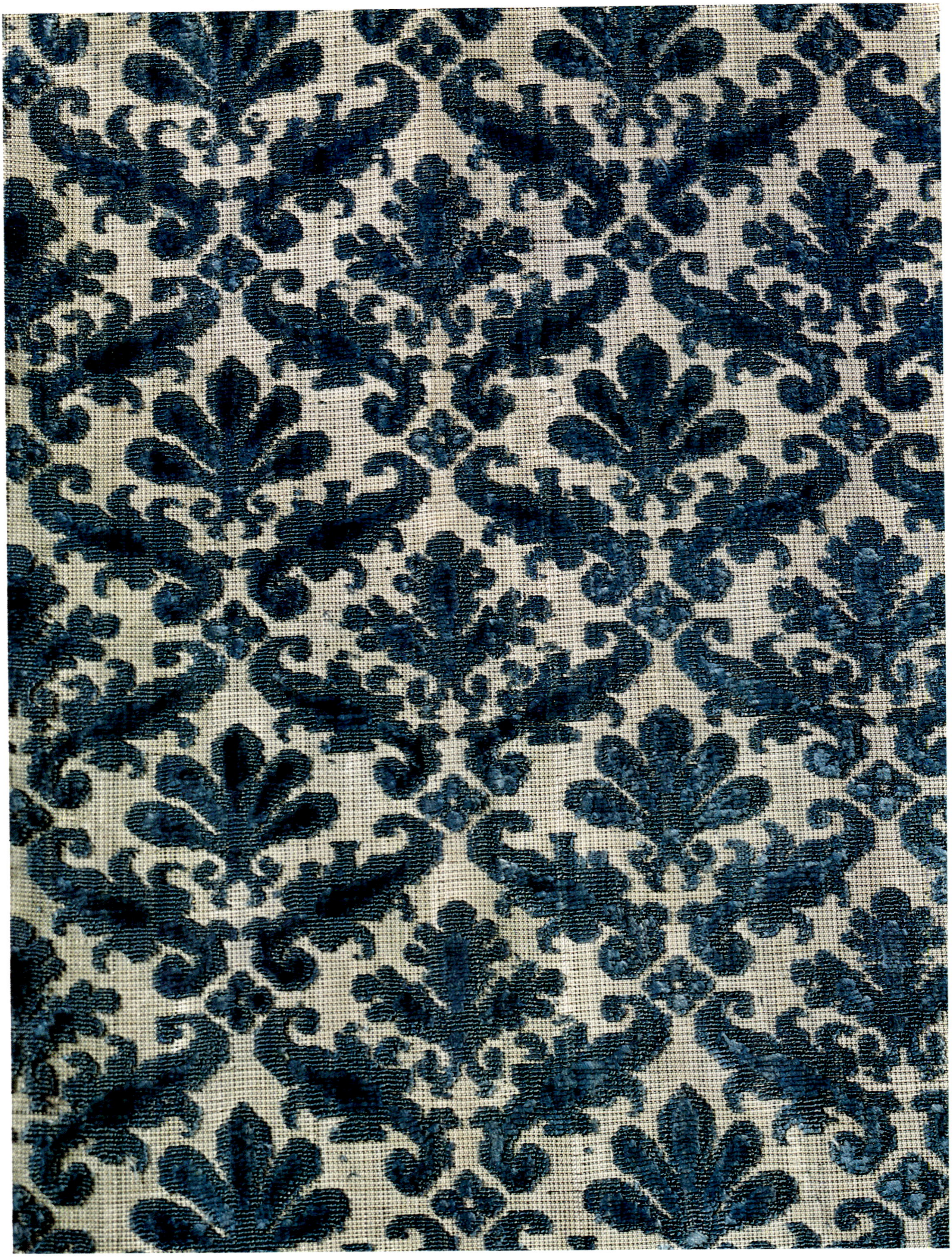

46

51

60

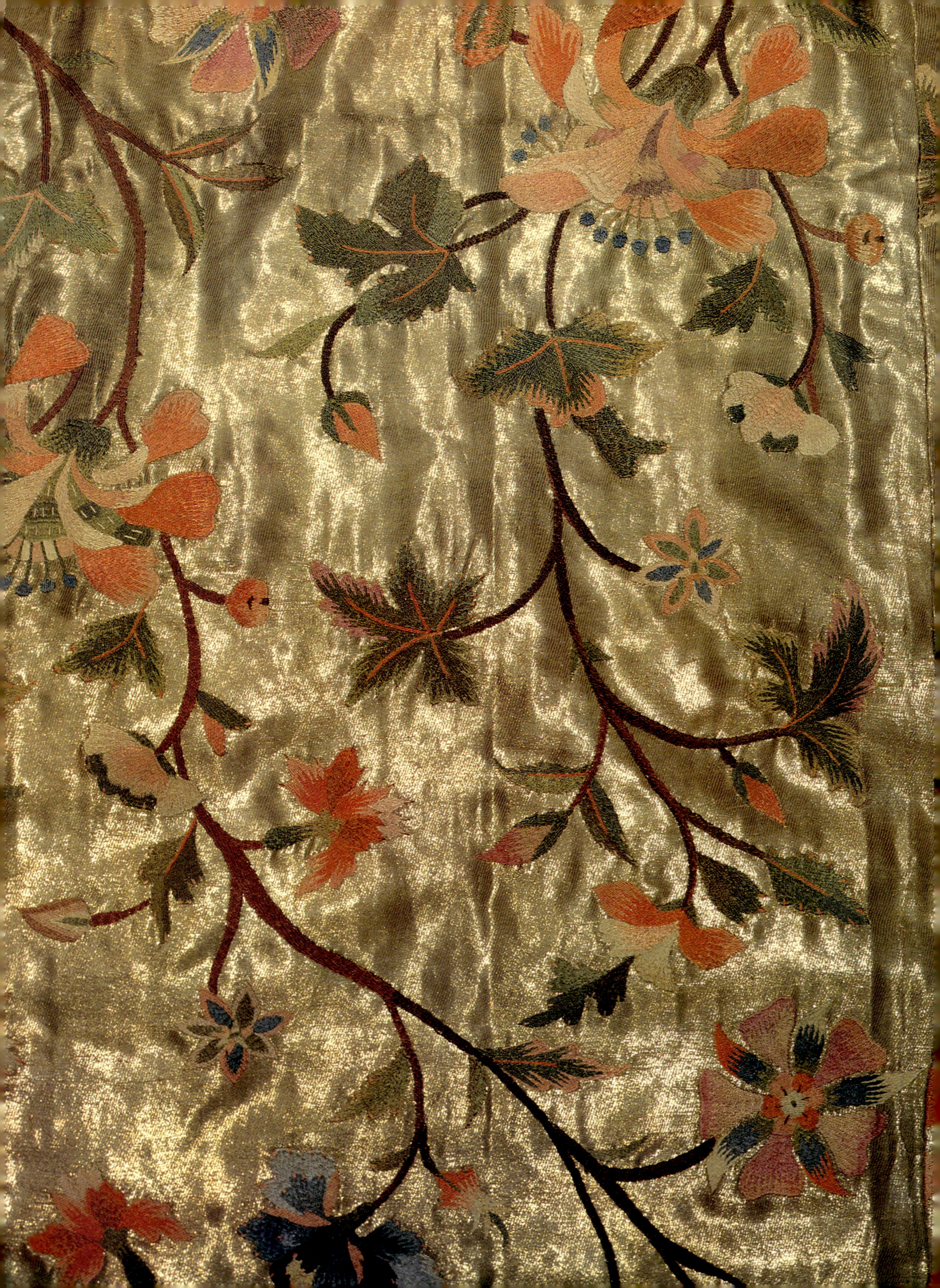

66

67

68

70

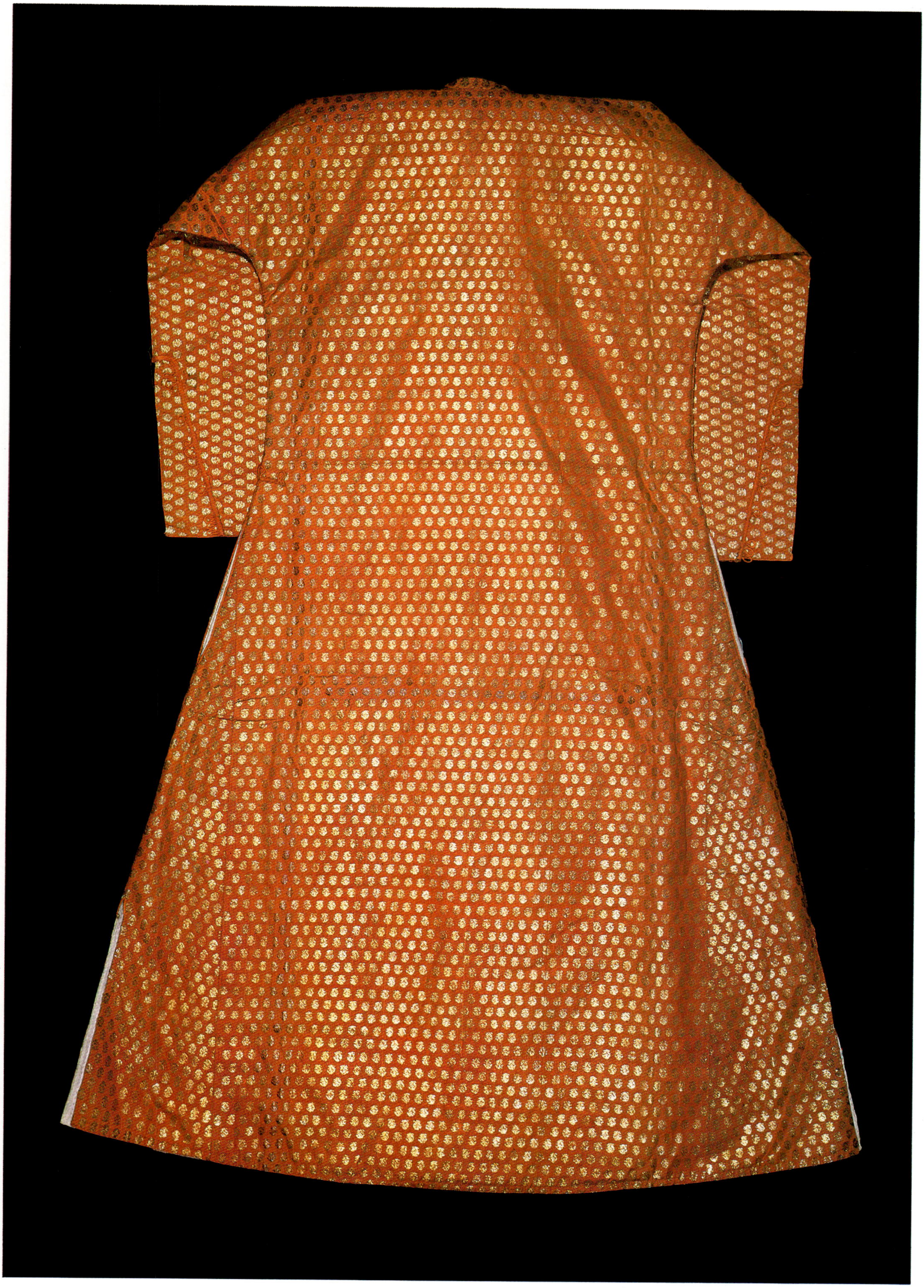

74

80

81

82

83

CAPTIONS AND NOTES TO ILLUSTRATIONS

continued from page 48

21 Short-sleeved kaftan of Murād III (1574–95), of heavy brown satin with appliqué of lamé (*serāser*) crescents and stylized tulips, probably late sixteenth century; 13/195. Length 148·5 cm.
The pattern is identical to that of the kaftan (*ill. 51*) associated with Süleymān III (1687–91), though the length is different. Though far too few garments associated with any particular Sultan have been identified to make it possible to speak of individual taste in fabrics, it is highly probable that some designs were popular and periodically revived.

22 Long-sleeved ceremonial kaftan, associated with Sultan Ibrāhīm (1640–8), of heavy white satin with satin appliqué of triple spots or crescents and single tiger-stripes in crimson satin, seventeenth century; 13/486. Length 170 cm.

23 Long-sleeved ceremonial kaftan, bearing a label stating that it belonged to Murād III (1574–95), of compound tabby with gold or silver metal thread, with sharply undulating scrolls of slashed tulip buds and leaves which recall tiger-stripes, in crimson pile velvet, lining partially of stamped grey satin, sixteenth century; 13/216. Length 150 cm.
□ *The Anatolian Civilisations*, E 135.

24 Long-sleeved kaftan, associated with Murād III (1574–95), worn before his accession, of faded red silk velvet, later sixteenth century; 13/199. Length 92 cm.

25 Long-sleeved ceremonial kaftan, associated with Murād III (1574–95), of white silk with medallions edged with carnations and peacock feathers and filled with cloud-scrolls, and with crescents in cinnamon silk enclosing stars, sixteenth century; 13/221. Length 151 cm.
The kaftan was probably partly fur-lined originally.
□ Tahsin Öz, *Turkish Textiles and Velvets*, Plate XXXI; *The Anatolian Civilisations*, E 111.

26 Gown, associated with Murād III (1574–95), of dull-blue rucked silk, with triple-spot motifs printed in silver, lined with white satin and red silk printed with silver spots, sixteenth century; 13/198. Length 132·5 cm.
Cf. Tahsin Öz, *Turkish Textiles and Velvets*, Plate XVI (with a jacket in similar materials); *The Anatolian Civilisations*, E 116, where it is stated that the robe is tailored for a (rather stout) woman, not a man, so that the label attributing it to Murād III must be disregarded.

27 (and detail) Long-sleeved ceremonial kaftan, associated with Meḥmed III (1595–1603), voided velvet on a gold brocaded ground with elongated medallions of slender acanthus volutes and pomegranates, Prunus blossoms, tulip buds and stylized chinoiserie lotus, probably Italian later sixteenth century; 13/834. Length 154 cm.
It has generally been accepted that the fabric is Italian, though the dates given it have varied widely: 'Italy *c.* 1500' of a piece in the Musée Historique de Tissus, Lyons (Raymond Cox, *Les Soieries d'art*, Plate 54/ii); 'Italy, sixteenth century' of a piece in Berlin (*Encyclopaedia of Textiles*, Plate 78).

28 (and detail) Short-sleeved kaftan of Meḥmed III (1595–1603), of brocaded velvet, with alternating stylized floral compositions rising from a crown in black and faded pink or red, Italian, later sixteenth century; 13/835. Length 160 cm.
For very close parallels, in the Musée Historique de Tissus, Lyons, and in the Gewebesammlung, Krefeld, see Raymond Cox, *Les Soieries d'art*, Plate 56/iv and especially 56/vi; *Encyclopaedia of Textiles*, Plates 88–9.

29 Short-sleeved child's kaftan (front and back view), associated with the childhood of Aḥmed I, of brocaded crimson silk with an ogival pattern employing feathery composite leaves, triple spots, adaptations of Venetian crowns and cardoons, lined partially with a stamped dull golden-yellow satin, later sixteenth century; 13/277. Length 67·5 cm.
□ Tahsin Öz, *Türk Kumaş ve Kadifeleri* I, Plate XXXVII, accepts the attribution.

30 Short-sleeved boy's kaftan (back view), associated with Aḥmed I, of crimson silk brocade, with bold serrated leaves and heavy undulating stems with floral filling on a ground of tulips and stylized foliate motifs, late sixteenth century; 13/267. Length 76 cm.
The design is a simplified version of the pattern seen in *ill. 3*. Tahsin Öz, *Türk Kumaş ve Kadifeleri* II, Plate XLI, states that the kaftan is from the tomb of Aḥmed I. He illustrates a similarly patterned fragment, on a different-coloured ground (ibid., Plate XLII).

31 (and detail) Ceremonial long-sleeved kaftan, associated with Aḥmed I (1603–17), gold-brocaded crimson velvet with large palmate medallions in heavy rope-like borders with smaller palmate medallions attached, the broad collar lined with stamped green satin, seventeenth century; 13/337. Length 162 cm.
The designs are typically Venetian, of the sixteenth–seventeenth century, but were much imitated in contemporary Spain.

32 (and detail) Short-sleeved youth's kaftan (back view), associated with Aḥmed I (1603–17), cloth of gold or silver (*serāser*) with a pattern of crescents and light stylized foliate sprays in faded pink and green, seventeenth century; 13/265. Length 113 cm.

33 Short-sleeved youth's kaftan (back view), from the tomb of Sultan Aḥmed I (1603–17), crimson brocaded medallion silk with filling of stylized cypresses and florists' flowers, seventeenth century; 13/266. Length 89 cm.
□ *The Anatolian Civilisations*, E 143.

34 Short-sleeved kaftan (back view), from the tomb of Aḥmed I, medallion brocade with fat palmette motifs formed of thin serrated leaves on a ground of slender tulips, late sixteenth century; 13/268. Length 71·5 cm.
For the odd treatment of the palmette cf. a piece in the Musée Historique de Tissus, Lyons, attributed to Italy, sixteenth century (Raymond Cox, *Les Soieries d'art*, Plate 61/iii), featuring a wheatsheaf motif with fat ears of corn.

35 Long-sleeved kaftan of heavy ribbed crimson satin, associated with Şehzade Ḳāsim, a son of Aḥmed I, seventeenth century; 13/269. Length 158 cm.

36 Child's quilted gown, with a label stating that it belonged to Ḫānzāde Sulṭān, a daughter of Aḥmed I (1603–17), striped satin, lined partially with bright-blue satin, early seventeenth century; 13/275. Length 54 cm.

37 Quilted over-garment (*ḥırḳa*), attributed to Şehzade Ḳāsim, a son of Aḥmed I (1603–17), striped silk (*cānfes*), seventeenth century; 13/263. Length 84 cm.

38 Short-sleeved kaftan, traditionally attributed to ʿOsmān III (1754–7), but possibly of ʿOsmān II (1618–22), silk brocade with heavy undulating stems bearing stylized pomegranates and cypresses or pine-cones in a characteristically sixteenth-century design and colour-scheme; 13/584. Length 137·5 cm.
Concerning the problem of dating, cf. Tahsin Öz, *Türk Kumaş ve Kadifeleri* II, Plates CXXVI-VII (with a seventeenth-century attribution), and *The Anatolian Civilisations*, E 140 (with the same design on a cream ground, and a sixteenth-century attribution). Either the kaftan is mistakenly attributed, therefore, or an earlier silk has been re-used. In general there are too few attributable garments to make it possible to speak of a particular Sultan's personal taste, or even of the fashion of a particular decade or decades. Fashion was obviously, however, of some importance for designs.

39 (and detail) Short-sleeved kaftan of ʿOsmān II (1618–22), showing the bloodstains from his assassination, lamé or cloth of gold, embroidered with stylized floral sprigs in various colours, early seventeenth century; 13/365. Length 148 cm.
□ Tahsin Öz, *Türk Kumaş ve Kadifeleri* II, Plate XLIV, and compare Plate XLV.

40 Long-sleeved ceremonial kaftan, associated with ʿOsmān II (1618–22), of raw silk, with a design of feathery leaves, foliate trails and large circles treated as crescents filled with stars, seventeenth century; 13/357. Length 154 cm.
□ Tahsin Öz, *Türk Kumaş ve Kadifeleri* II, Plate XLIII.

41 Long-sleeved ceremonial kaftan, associated with Murād IV (1623–40), of white raw silk, with a pattern of gold and green pointed medallions of sprays of tulips and other florists' flowers enclosing lobed rosettes, seventeenth century; 13/470. Length 151 cm.
□ Tahsin Öz, *Türk Kumaş ve Kadifeleri* II, Plate XLVI.

42 Short-sleeved kaftan (back view), probably belonging to ʿOsmān II (1618–22), brocaded velvet on a lamé or cloth of gold ground, with lobed medallions filled with stylized lotus and spiralling foliate scrolls in blue velvet, seventeenth century; 13/360. Length 135 cm.
The fabric is almost certainly of European manufacture. Compare a brocaded velvet, Italian, early sixteenth century, in the Museum für Kunsthandwerk, Dresden (*Encyclopaedia of Textiles*, Plate 71); and a Spanish gold brocade, sixteenth century (O. von Falke, *Kunstgeschichte der Seidenweberei* [Berlin 1913] II, No. 563).

43 Long-sleeved ceremonial kaftan, associated with Murād IV (1623–40), of crimson, gold-brocaded velvet, with ogival design and filling of heavy foliate motifs or rinceaux, the collar spreading and lined with crimson satin and the lining of the robe itself being partly of satin coloured deep blue, Italian or Spanish, seventeenth century; 13/839. Length 146·5 cm.

44 Long-sleeved ceremonial kaftan, associated with Murād IV (1623–40), gold-brocaded crimson satin with triple spots and tiger-stripes enhanced with pale blue, seventeenth century; 13/408. Length 155 cm.
Tahsin Öz, *Türk Kumaş ve Kadifeleri* II, Plate XLVII, identifies a particularly broad kaftan of this type, with a similar flaring collar, as Murād IV's.

45 (and detail) Kaftan (back view), associated with Murād IV (1623–40), brocade, probably Spanish, with stylized lotuses and heavy scrolls, seventeenth century; 13/838. Length 137·5 cm.
For similar Spanish brocades cf. O. von Falke, *Kunstgeschichte der Seidenweberei* (Berlin 1913) II, No. 562; Raymond Cox, *Les Soieries d'art*, Plate 67/iii.

46 (and detail) Short-sleeved kaftan, associated with Murād IV (1623–40), brocaded blue velvet with voided pile on lamé ground, with all-over foliate lozenge design, Italian, seventeenth century; 13/413. Length 105 cm.
For an almost identical silk velvet with voided pile, Italian, seventeenth century, in the Gewebesammlung, Krefeld, cf. *Encyclopaedia of Textiles*, Plate 87. There is a similar velvet, identified as 'Italian, sixteenth century' in the Musée Historique de Tissus, Lyons (Raymond Cox, *Les Soieries d'art*, Plate 63/v).

47 Short-sleeved kaftan, associated with Sultan Ibrāhīm (1640–8), brocade of silver-wrapped yellow silk thread, with a pattern of pointed oval medallions with rosebuds and other florists' flowers, seventeenth century; 13/489. Length 150 cm.

48 (and detail) Long-sleeved ceremonial kaftan, erroneously associated with Meḥmed the Conqueror (1451–81), of lamé or cloth of gold (*serāser*), with enormous pointed oval serrated medallions, filled with fan-like (*yelpaze*) carnations, with stylized crowns and blossoms between the medallions, lined partially with crimson satin, later sixteenth or early seventeenth century; 13/9. Length 159·5 cm.
Neither in design nor in dimensions does this kaftan fit with other kaftans associated with or attributed to Meḥmed II. The grounds for the existing attribution are not stated. If there was a label, 'Meḥmed', this must relate to Meḥmed III (1595–1603), or possibly Meḥmed IV (1648–87).
☐ L. Mackie in E. Atıl (ed.), *Turkish Art*. No. 210.

49 Long-sleeved short ceremonial kaftan, associated with Meḥmed IV (1648–87), of gold-brocaded crimson velvet with heavy undulating stems of stylized pomegranates and dense foliate ornament of serrated leaves and cardoons, Spanish or Italian, seventeenth century; 13/500. Length 109 cm.
The closest parallel is in the Musée Historique de Tissus, Lyons, attributed to Spain, sixteenth century (Raymond Cox, *Les Soieries d'art*, Plate 57/ii).

50 Long-sleeved ceremonial kaftan, associated with Süleymān III (1687–91), lamé or cloth of gold (*serāser*), striped bright blue, lined partially with faded rose satin, later seventeenth century; 13/512. Length 159 cm.

51 Short-sleeved kaftan, associated with Süleymān III (1687–91), crimson satin with appliqué of crescents and stylized tulips in lamé or cloth of gold (*serāser*), seventeenth century; 13/514. Length 164 cm.
☐ L. Mackie in E. Atıl (ed.), *Turkish Art*, No. 212.

52 Long-sleeved ceremonial kaftan, associated with Aḥmed II (1691–3), with quilted lining and low collar, ivory silk with self-coloured pattern of sprigged flowers, seventeenth century; 13/525. Length 150·5 cm.

53 Short-sleeved kaftan, associated with Aḥmed II (1691–3), of ivory satin with circular medallions in olive-brown containing triple spots, lined partially with stamped crimson satin, seventeenth century; 13/522. Length 134 cm.

54 Short-sleeved kaftan, associated with Aḥmed III (1703–30), cloth of gold or silver, with contrasting medallions outlined in bright pink with stylized pomegranates between fat serrated leaves, *c*. 1700; 13/532. Length 139 cm.
Compare *The Anatolian Civilisations*, E289; *Encyclopaedia of Textiles*, Plate 279 (Vienna Private Collection, possibly that now in the Museum of Fine Arts, Boston) and Plate 272 for similar leaves, with an attribution, 'Turkey, sixteenth century'. There is further confusion since Tahsin Öz, *Türk Kumaş ve Kadifeleri* II, Plate LVI, accepts the attribution to Aḥmed III, but in his *Turkish Textiles and Velvets* (see Bibliographical note below, p. 211), in the case of Plates I, II and IV, implausibly attributes such textiles – doubtless on the basis of misplaced or misleading labels – to the fourteenth or early fifteenth century. For another pattern with similar leaves but a much fuller ground cf. *Türk Kumaş ve Kadifeleri* II, Plate LVI.

55 Long-sleeved kaftan, associated with Maḥmūd I (1730–54), of brown silk velvet, partially lined with deep-blue satin, eighteenth century; 13/557. Length 136 cm.

56 Short-sleeved kaftan, associated with Maḥmūd I (1730–54), of heavy crimson satin, with appliqué triangles of ivory satin with a stamped medallion design, eighteenth century; 13/558. Length 168 cm.
To judge by other Kaftans associated with Maḥmud I (*ills. 55, 57*), this example seems to be far too long.

57 (and detail) Long-sleeved heavy gown belonging to Maḥmūd I (1730–54), striped blue silk (*selīmīye*) with stylized floral scrolls, eighteenth century, 13/554. Length 125 cm.
The gown bears a label dated 25 Rabīʿ I 1171/7 December 1757, stating that on that date the wardrobe of the late Sultan Maḥmūd was registered in the Harem of the Palace by ʿAlī Ağa.
☐ Tahsin Öz, *Türk Kumaş ve Kadifeleri* II, Plate LVII.

58 Long-sleeved ceremonial kaftan, very probably belonging to Muṣṭafā III (1757–74), of deep-blue lamé or cloth of silver, with elaborate frogging of crimson-bordered silver braid on the chest, eighteenth century; 13/595. Length 117·5 cm.

59 Long-sleeved under-kaftan, associated with Muṣṭafā III (1757–74), of ivory watered silk, eighteenth century; 13/589. Length 143 cm.

60 Quilted child's kaftan, belonging to Fāṭma Sulṭān, a daughter of Muṣṭafā III (1757–74), faded red silk, resist dyed with an all-over lozenge design, eighteenth century; 13/807. Length 48 cm.

61 Light gown (*entari*), belonging to Fāṭma Sulṭān, a daughter of Muṣṭafā III (1757–74), of flowered lamé, the flowers being stylized double poppies, a favourite eighteenth-century silk design from Mughal India to Poland, eighteenth century; 13/805. Length 66 cm.

62 Long-sleeved gown, believed to have belonged to Fāṭma Sulṭān, a daughter of Muṣṭafā III, of plain dark-blue moiré silk with trimmings of gold braid, eighteenth century; 13/803. Length 105 cm.

63 Girl's woollen coat, made for Fāṭma Sulṭān, a daughter of Muṣṭafā III (1757–74), showing the fur lining, with panels of silk and embroidery in metal thread, eighteenth century; 13/814. Length 66 cm.

64 (and detail) Loose gown (*entari*), belonging to Fāṭma Sulṭān, a daughter of Muṣṭafā III (1757–74), of silver lamé (*serāser*), with embroidered appliqué of floral motifs deriving from chintz in coloured silks, eighteenth century; 13/804. Length 95 cm.

65 (and detail) Gown belonging to Fāṭma Sulṭān, a daughter of Muṣṭafā III (1757–74), dark-blue silk with overlying all-over arabesques in silver thread, eighteenth century; 13/815. Length 93 cm.

66 Gown (*entari*), belonging to Fāṭma Sulṭān, a daughter of Muṣṭafā III (1757–74), of red *selīmīye* silk with an all-over pattern of rosettes in gold thread, eighteenth century; 13/812. Length 95 cm.
☐ *The Anatolian Civilisations*, E 290.

67 Short-sleeved girl's dress, bearing a label attributing it to a certain 'Ṣāliḥa Sulṭān', *selīmīye* silk with all-over minute design in gold thread, trimmed with heavy gold braid, eighteenth century; 13/819. Length 72 cm.
Tahsin Öz, *Türk Kumaş ve Kadifeleri* II, Plate LXI, identifies 'Ṣāliḥa Sulṭān' with a daughter of ʿAbdü'l-Ḥamīd I (1774–89). So far, however, that suggestion has not been corroborated.

68 Long-sleeved girl's dress, bearing a label attributing it to 'Ṣāliḥa Sulṭān', of *selīmīye* silk with an all-over minute pattern, heavily trimmed with gold braid, probably eighteenth century; 13/818. Length 72·5 cm.

69 Loose child's robe, belonging to 'Ṣāliḥa Sulṭān', minute patterned *selīmīye* silk, with trimming of gold braid, eighteenth century; 13/816. Length 72 cm.

70 Robe, labelled 'Ṣāliḥa Sulṭān', with a self design of heavy flowers and leaves, probably French, eighteenth century; 13/820. Length 71 cm.
The trimmings are of gold embroidery. Cf. a French silk, 'Louis XIV', in the Musée Historique de Tissus, Lyons (Raymond Cox. *Les Soieries d'art*, Plate 71/iii).

71 Garment of an unidentified Sultan, of red *selīmīye* silk with all-over pattern of stylized foliate motifs in gold thread; 13/808, eighteenth century. Length 92 cm.

72 Loose gown (*entari*), associated with Rukīye Sulṭān (a so far unidentified princess), of golden-brown relief pile velvet on gold lamé (*serāser*), eighteenth century; 13/795. Length 81·5 cm.

73 Cloak belonging to ʿAbdü'l-Ḥamīd I (1774–89), of scarlet watered satin, with trimmings and frogging of metal thread, eighteenth century; 13/608. Length 114·5 cm.

74 Long-sleeved fine scarlet woollen cloth kaftan made for Selīm III (1789–1807), late eighteenth century; 13/623. Length 119 cm.
Among the Westernizing reforms of Selīm III was the equipment of his Janissary troops with European-type uniforms of woollen cloth. This came mostly from the big Jewish contractors at Salonike and other Balkan towns.

75 Striped crimson silk robe of Selīm III (1789–1807), *c.*1800; 13/626. Length 110·5 cm.

76 Kaftan (back view), probably worn by Muṣṭafā IV (1807–8) as a child, silver or gold lamé with roses, lined partially with faded pink silk, nineteenth century; 13/631. Length 74 cm.
Cf. *The Anatolian Civilisations*, E288, though there without an attribution. The pattern of roses is close to that of a late eighteenth-century French silk in Krefeld, Gewebesammlung (*Encyclopaedia of Textiles*, Plate 222).

77 Long-sleeved gown, worn by Maḥmūd II (1808–39) before his accession, sprigged silk with metal thread, nineteenth century; 13/669. Length 104 cm.

78 Short-sleeved kaftan belonging to Maḥmūd II (1808–39), of chestnut moiré silk, lined partially with olive satin and with a pattern of stylized chinoiserie lotus medallions in tarnished metal thread, nineteenth century; 13/644. Length 150 cm.

79 Short-sleeved kaftan of Maḥmūd II (1808–39), striped silk with metal thread, nineteenth century; 13/670. Length 148 cm.

80 Jacket, worn by ʿAbdü'l-Mecīd (1839–61) before his accession, scarlet woollen cloth with gold-braid trimmings, nineteenth century; 13/715. Length 44 cm.

81 Jacket, worn by ʿAbdü'l-Mecīd (1839–61) before his accession, black woollen cloth with heavy gold-braid trimmings and frogging, nineteenth century; 13/716. Length 47·5 cm.

82 Frock-coat (*setre*), made for ʿAbdü'l-Mecīd (1839–61), black woollen cloth with heavy trimming and frogging of gold braid and scarlet collar and cuffs, nineteenth century; 13/848. Length 106 cm.

83 Woollen coat, made for Murād V (1876), black with scarlet trimmings and heavy gold and silver braiding; 13/699. Length 105 cm.

84 Fine woollen shirt, made for ʿAbdü'l-ʿAzīz (1861–76); 13/701. Length 90 cm.

85 Uniform coat made for Meḥmed V Reşād (1909–18), navy wool with scarlet trimmings and heavy gold braiding; 13/731. Length 104 cm.

PART II
Embroideries

Turkish embroideries: historical documentation

THE collection of embroideries, dating from the sixteenth to the twentieth century, in the Topkapı Saray forms one of the most important sections of the museum. They are from the Treasury (Hazine) and other parts of the Palace and came to light when the buildings were being transformed into a museum in the years following the Revolution. Yet others are from the Royal tombs, choice pieces covering the cenotaphs erected over the graves of Sultans, princes and the Royal ladies. Most of the finest of the sixteenth- and seventeenth-century embroideries are from this source. In addition to cenotaph covers, they include handkerchiefs, ladies' head-bands to keep their head-dress in position, sashes, turban-covers, head-covers and towels (*makrama*). The collection was considerably augmented by purchase in the 1930s, the additions being mostly eighteenth- and nineteenth-century pieces.

Embroideries have played an important part in Turkish life, especially in the life of the Palace. This was noted by an English visitor in the 1840s:[1]

> Muslim and cotton handkerchiefs . . . are employed less, possibly, for the purposes for which such articles are applied in Europe than for that of folding up money, linen and other things. In the houses of the great men there is always a *makrama başı*, whose principal duty is to take care of these and other similar articles. No object, great or small, is conveyed from one person to another; no present is made – even fees to medical men, unless folded in a handkerchief, embroidered cloth or piece of gauze. The more rich the envelope the higher the compliment to the receiver.

Again,

> . . . when the Sultan honours individuals by bestowing upon them a gift the present, whether consisting of fruits, sweet meats or wearing apparel, is always enclosed in an embroidered cloth, kerchief or gauze, in the same manner as is practised in the transmission of letters.

The range of embroideries is even greater than this account implies. From costumes to floor-coverings, from swaddling bands to shrouds, from brides' trousseaux to battle standards and tent-work there was no aspect of life in which they were out of place. Their importance derives partly from Turkish tradition and taste, but partly also from a general human love of decoration. The absence of many Western types of furniture from Ottoman houses and palaces is also an important factor in the high esteem in which they were held, for they were an essential in interior decoration. The main item of furniture in Turkish houses, even in palaces, was the divan. This was often on a raised platform and would be strewn with bolsters and cushions with embroidered covers. But the floor-coverings (the vogue for carpets, for which Turkey was famous in sixteenth-century Europe, was slow in developing in Ottoman Turkey), window- and door-curtains, fire-screens or hearth-curtains would also often have been embroidered. Such furnishings were not confined to the Palace, however. There is a list, dated 1 Cumādā I 1018–late Zilḳ'ade 1026/2 August 1609–late November 1617,[2] of the furnishings of the Sultan's box (*maḥfil-i laṭīf*) in the mosque of Sultan Aḥmed in Istanbul, which specifies bolsters of pale-blue brocade and (embroidered) curtains of twill (*boğasi*) and green or red curtains of woollen cloth with embroidered silk fastenings, all at considerable cost. The furnishings may have been so lavish because their function was partly to screen the Sultan at the Friday prayers and to protect him from assassination, though they must also have been necessary to keep out the draught during the bitter Istanbul winter. But they would also add to the ceremony, giving the famous Blue Mosque a brilliance and splendour which it is now difficult to imagine.

The earliest mention of embroideries in the Palace is a register of the Treasury (possibly only a partial register) of Bāyazīd II, dated 910/1505.[3] Among the many precious objects listed there are embroidered cushions and bolsters (for thrones and divans), some with metal thread and some with coloured silks. There were also mats or floor-coverings (*nihāli*), one of them with a leopard-skin centre worked with silver or gold thread and with a surround of grey Italian velvet fit for the Doge (*dūcevī*). Also listed are door- and window-curtains with silver rings to hang them by, towels, napkins and wrappers (*bohça*), and bedspreads or quilt-covers. Their presence demonstrates that the surviving pieces of embroidery, none earlier than the mid-sixteenth century, are the product of an already well established tradition.

In the Topkapı Saray Archives there is a register, dated Rabīʿ II 932/February–March 1526, of craftsmen then in the employ of the Palace. This includes the *cemāʿat-i zerdūzān*, a group of five embroiderers in gold, together with a note of their origins, the wages they were paid and the date they came into the Sultan's service:

Bülbül – 8 akçe a day, originally from Tabriz, though he had worked for a time in Amasya, taken into employment on 25 Muḥarram 926/17 January 1520;
Hemdem, a Bosnian – 7½ akçe a day, presented by Hocazade Meḥmed Paşa to Selīm I in 926/1519–20;
Ḳāsim Üngürüs, a Hungarian – 14½ akçe a day, brought back, evidently from Budapest, by Süleymān the Magnificent;
Murād – 10½ akçe a day, taken into Palace employment in 929/1522–3, recruited for his dexterity;
Beşāret, a Georgian – 10½ akçe, a day, from Tabriz, a slave of the Safavid Shāh Ismāʿīl, taken into Palace employment in 929/1522–3.

Whether they were all slaves is unclear: the majority of the Palace craftsmen seem to have been free. And though their very different origins may have cancelled one another out, the fact that two of them had had experience in Tabriz suggests strongly that Safavid gold embroidery was much to Ottoman taste.

This 1526 register and later registers of Palace craftsmen (*ehl-i ḥiref*) leave it in no doubt that the gold-embroiderers were all men. This may well be a direct survival from Roman times. Then, as at the Byzantine court, gold-embroiderers in the Imperial workshops – though called *gynaeciarii* (employees of the women's quarters) – were invariably men.[5] One must assume that the *cemāʿat-i zerdūzān* worked only in gold, for it is difficult to imagine how a mere five men could have handled Palace demand for embroideries of all sorts. The numbers of craftsmen, moreover, fluctuate markedly. In a Palace register of the late 1550s, listing rewards to craftsmen for the gifts they presented to the Sultan on the great feasts of the Muslim year, only one embroiderer is mentioned; no gold embroidery appears in the lists of gifts; and the only embroidery mentioned is buttons, presented by three button-makers (*düğmeci*).[6]

As regards the work of silk-embroiderers outside the Palace, an interesting report to one of the Royal ladies has survived. The Palace had ordered seven bedspreads, each 5 *endaze* (1 *endaze* = 65 cm approx.) long. The ten women commissioned to do the work had returned it saying that it was too fine and beyond their skill; no others could be found to do it. The work must have been to execute designs supplied by the Palace, which doubtless also prescribed the colours to be used and the treatment of the motifs. The report, the content of which is not entirely clear, states that for each bedspread, which would have been almost 3·25 m long, the women had been allotted 450 to 500 *dirham* of silk thread, which would have weighed almost 1·5 kg. This gives a graphic idea of the fineness of the embroidery and the laboriousness of the work, which would have taken an embroiderer working all out not less than a year to complete.

As far as the Palace embroideries were concerned, therefore, those using principally gold thread were made in the Palace workshop by men, whereas silk embroidery was executed, doubtless under strict control, by women on commission either in the Harem or outside the Palace. The gold and silver thread was also made outside the Palace and was available to the public. In times of scarcity the authorities could step in to forbid its manufacture, as is shown by an edict dated Receb 1128/July 1716[8] which explicitly states that there was a shortage of silver at the Mint, reinforcing the prohibition by recourse to sumptuary restrictions: but the prohibition doubtless did not apply to work within the Palace. Curiously, however, the authorities did little or nothing to control the quality of the thread. George I Rákóczy, Prince of Transylvania, who in the 1630s made large purchases of gold and silver thread in Istanbul, was more than once warned by his correspondents in Istanbul that the quality might not be satisfactory; and indeed one consignment was returned since the silver was found to be debased with copper.[8]

Nor did the Palace have a monopoly in gold- or silver-embroidery. Light articles like handkerchiefs or towels were a cottage industry in Istanbul: the work in coloured silks was often enhanced with metal thread. Heavy embroidery on satin or velvet, such as coverlets or bolster-cases, could be ordered from professional embroiderers, or from the Venetian merchants in Galata who kept stocks of these ready made. The maker of the embroidered quivers ordered by the Hungarian prince Gabriel Bethlen in the 1620s had, moreover, to be provided with all the basic materials – the ground fabric; the precious yarns; cotton for padding the raised motifs; and pearls and semi-precious stones. Bethlen's accounts also mention a craftsman who was employed to draw the pattern on the ground fabric: he received separate payment and therefore very probably had his own workshop.[9] Sometimes, as a letter sent by Stephen Szalánczi to George I Rákóczy from Istanbul shows, foreigners could specify the patterns themselves, though they would almost certainly have been to Ottoman Turkish taste:[10]

> We did not dare to have the flowers embroidered for the saddle blanket, as, according to the flowers which Your Excellency wishes, it would cost a great deal. The flowers are large, thus a lot of skofium [gold or silver thread] would be needed for them. If Your Excellency so orders, they will be embroidered quickly.

Further information on the Palace embroideries relates to the cloths of the Arz Odası (the Audience Chamber) in the Topkapı Saray, where the Sultan sat in audience or received foreign ambassadors and where the furnishings were appropriately magnificent and showy. One of the best descriptions of these is by Jean Baptiste Tavernier in his account of his travels to India via Turkey and Persia in the early 1670s. He visited the Treasury of the Topkapı Saray, where the Arz Odası cloths were kept, and saw the festival throne (*Bayram tahtı*):[11]

> The Throne, which is rich enough, is in the manner of an Altar, and it is brought into that Hall [sc. the Arz Odası] only upon those days, whereon the Grand Seignor is willing to give Audience to Ambassadors, and when the new *Chan* of the lesser *Tartary*, whom he has chosen to govern there, comes to receive the Investiture of his Kingdom, and to take the accustomed Oath. The back-side of the Throne, is set against a partitition erected for that purpose, which is not above half a foot higher than it, and 'tis that keeps in the cushions which are behind the Grand Seignor.
>
> There are in the Treasury-Chamber . . . several very sumptuous Coverings purposely made to cover the aforesaid Throne: and they are so large, that they reach down to the ground on three sides of it, that is to say, before, on the right hand, and on the left: for as to the back part, it is, as I told you, fastened to the partition. The most Magnificent of all those Coverings is of a black Velvet, with an Embroydery of great Pearls, whereof some are long, and others round, and in the form of Buttons. There is another of white Velvet, set out with an Embroydery of Rubies and Emeralds, most whereof are set in Beazils, or Collets, the better to keep them in. There is a third, of a Violet-colour'd Velvet, embroyder'd with Turqueses and Pearls. The three others, which are next in esteem to these, are also of Velvets of different Colours, with a rich Embroydery of Gold. And the two last are of a Gold-Brokado, which have also their particular Beauty and sumptuousness. The Throne is adorn'd with one of these coverings, according to the Grand Seignor's respect to the Sovereign, whose Embassy he receives; and he levels his own Magnificence to that of the Prince whom he would honour.

Other seventeenth-century European accounts of the Arz Odası bear out Tavernier's admiration. We also learn from them that the floor of the chamber was strewn with gold-embroidered 'carpets' of great worth, some writers indicating that these were actually embroideries too.

These accounts by European travellers and diplomats are corroborated by documents in the Topkapı Saray Archives. For example, a register dated 1091/1680–1[12] of the Palace Treasury lists the cloths, their colours and the type of embroidery used for each. For special occasions the Arz Odası was decorated with no less than sixty pieces of embroidery. Six skirts (*etek*), five cushions and fifteen bolsters were used for the throne alone. These were sewn with emeralds, rubies and pearls of various sizes and worked with gold thread. To cover the floor there were twelve mats (*nihāli*) of various sizes. They were mostly of solid couched gold embroidery (*zerdūz*), so densely worked that the material beneath could not be seen. There were also twelve wall- and window-hangings of crimson satin worked with *zerdūz*, a fire-screen or chimney-veil (*ocāḳ yaşmāğı*) and other cloths for the hearth, a cloth for a chair or stool and a mat for the doorway. On feast days an additional thirteen curtains were hung to decorate the exterior of the pavilion. The stuffs were brocade, velvet, Istanbul cloth of gold (*serāser*), generally crimson but occasionally green or purple, all sewn with gold thread, precious stones and pearls.

These magnificent embroideries had a sad fate. In the reign of ʿAbdü'l-Mecīd (1839–61) the Topkapı Saray ceased to be the Sultan's residence and was abandoned for palaces on the Bosphorus more in European taste. There was no longer any use for the Arz Odası. The wall-hangings, the curtains and the floor-coverings were all sent to the Mint to be melted down, yielding 88,345 kg of silver and 912 kg of gold. Not all of them by this late date may have been very old, of course; some of the cloths doubtless wore out or went out of fashion, and others were very probably given as presents to Sultans' daughters as wedding gifts. The few embroidered throne-cloths which have survived to the present day are mostly of cream-coloured Istanbul cloth of gold with couched gold embroidery and precious stones. There are also a few pieces of crimson velvet sewn with pearls. But these few pieces, which are now on exhibition in the Arz Odası, give only the faintest idea of the former magnificence and splendour of the Sultans in their heyday.

The embroideries for other parts of the Palace, floor-coverings, wall-hangings, cushion- and bolster-covers for the divans, were as precious as those for the Arz Odası. The 1680–1 register also gives considerable details on these. They also were worked with precious stones, spangles, metal thread and silver wire. There were, in addition, *sûzenî* (Persian, 'needlework') pieces, of Istanbul cloth of gold worked with silk thread. The register also refers to cradle-covers, mattress- and quilt-covers and mosquito nets, embroidered with metal thread and pearls, metal braid (*klaptan*) or couched gold thread.

Outside the Palace a register dated 1050/1640–1 fixing prices and profits for goods on the market in Istanbul (*es'ār defteri*) includes numerous types of embroidery, on leather as well as on fabrics, both heavy and light.[13] The latter include tent-work; curtains, of heavy woollen cloth embroidered with clouds; bed-spreads; fire-screen or chimney curtains of silk-embroidered English broadcloth (*londura*); floor-coverings of heavy cloth (*velense*), worked with blue or crimson Karaferye embroidery (from Beroia, in Western Thrace); cushion- and bolster-covers, both single- and double-sided; wrappers and bags. There were also numerous sorts of kerchiefs, collars and handkerchiefs at various prices. And there were the sorts of heavily embroidered articles which found such a heavy demand among the Hungarian and Transylvanian nobility – bow-cases and quivers worked with gold or silver thread; and saddles and saddle-cloths of embroidered velvet or leather. The quivers, for example, came in seven different sizes, ranging in price from 3,500 akçe down to 500 akçe each. This not only demonstrates the availability of fine work to anyone who was prepared to pay for it; it also shows how easy it was for the Palace to make up any shortfall in production by the Palace workshops by buying on the open market.

The fame of Turkish embroideries soon reached Western Europe. Marino Sanuto describes the appearance of Tomà Contarini before the Venetian Senate in 1528 bearing the Sultan's letter, 'molto larga, in un sacchetto di panno d'oro, alla turchescha, bollata con la testa del Signor,'[14] and evidently found this a novelty. But every Ottoman emissary abroad, and every foreign embassy received in audience by the Sultans was presented with some sort of embroidery – either stuffs, or bow-cases or quivers, or saddles, saddle-cloths or garnitures. These rapidly became collectors' pieces, and it is striking that the inventory of the collections of the Habsburg ruler Rudolf II made in 1607 in Prague, which is otherwise rich in Turkish, Persian and Indian objects, seems to have practically no embroideries in it. Among documented Ottoman presents is an interesting list of the lavish gifts from Maḥmūd I prepared for despatch to the Afghan conqueror, Nādir Shāh, just before his assassination in 1747 but never actually sent.[15] Among the lavishly decorated objects – valued at a total of 386,849 akçe – was a quiver, valued at 30,000 akçe, with a ground of green velvet with heavy gold embroidery, sewn with 3 large, 478 medium-sized and smaller diamonds, 2 large and 70 small rubies and spinels, 14 emeralds, and the straps, chains and rings all heavily embroidered and bejewelled, so that it was more a piece of goldsmith's work than of embroidery pure and simple. There were also a cushion of rich Istanbul golden silk (possibly cloth of gold), valued at 2,000 akçe, with 5 rubies, 120 emeralds, pearls and heavy gold embroidery; and a saddle of crimson velvet, with a star on the pommel, consisting of a large hexagonal emerald, in a surround of 71 diamonds and 73 rubies and sapphires, with similar stars on the crupper and smaller rosettes of diamonds, emeralds and sapphires all round in enamelled settings, the whole being valued at 40,000 akçe. The exceptional richness of the present suggests that Maḥmūd was attempting to buy Nādir Shāh off, for Iraq had suffered considerably from his attacks. As for Central and Eastern Europe, there is ample evidence from the early seventeenth century onwards that the Hungarian and Transylvanian nobility depended upon Istanbul not only for textiles of many sorts but also for embroideries on heavy ground fabrics (velvet, satin or broadcloth), that is, for saddles, saddle-cloths, bow-cases and quivers, embroidered wicker shields (*kalkan*) and even carriages and tents, both embroidered and appliqué.[16]

With the intensification of diplomatic relations in the later seventeenth century and, in particular, with the establishment of permanent foreign embassies in Istanbul, depictions of Ottoman society by Western painters became popular in Europe. This was the origin, very probably, of the fashion for Turkish costume in Europe in the early eighteenth century, in particular, for women's embroidered garments, kerchiefs, girdles and slippers. Lady Mary Wortley Montagu's description of the costume she ordered for herself is very striking:[17]

> The first piece of my dress is a pair of drawers, very full, that reach to my shoes, and conceal the legs more modestly than do your petticoats. They are of a thin rose-coloured damask, brocaded with silver flowers, my shoes are of white kid leather, embroidered with gold. Over this hangs my smock, of a fine white silk gauze, edged with embroidery. This smock has wide sleeves, hanging half-way down the arm, and is closed at the neck with a diamond button; but the shape and colour of the bosom well distinguished through it. The *antery* is a waistcoat, made close to the

> shape, of white or gold damask, with very long sleeves falling back, and fringed with deep gold fringe, and should have diamond or pearl buttons. My caftan, of the same stuff with my drawers, is a robe exactly fitted to my shape, and reaching to my feet, with very long strait falling sleeves. Over this is the girdle, of about four fingers broad, which all that can afford have entirely of diamonds or other precious stones; those who will not be at that expense, have it of exquisite embroidery on satin; but it must be fastened before with a clasp of diamonds. The *curdee* is a loose robe they throw off or put on according to the weather, being of a rich brocade (mine is green and gold) either lined with ermine or sables; the sleeves reach very little below the shoulders. The headdress is composed of a cap, called *talpock*, which is in winter of fine velvet embroidered with pearls and diamonds, and in summer of a light shining silver stuff. This is fixed on one side of the head, hanging a little way down with a gold tassel, and bound on, either with a circle of diamonds (as I have seen several) or a rich embroidered handkerchief . . .

This costume is illustrated, except for the diamonds, with surprising fidelity to this description in a portrait of a woman, who looks low, but may simply have been a Venetian or a Greek lady dressed up like Lady Mary, from the circle of Jean Baptiste Van Mour (1671–1737), an artist who was much in demand in Istanbul to record the Sultans' audiences given to foreign ambassadors to the Sublime Porte.[18]

Lady Mary Wortley Montagu also records a visit she made to Faṭma, the wife of Kedhuda Meḥmed Efendi at Edirne, who was similarly dressed in splendid embroidered garments: 'When I took my leave, two maids brought out a fine silver basket of embroidered handkerchiefs; she begged I would wear the richest for my sake, and gave the others to my woman and interpretess.'[19]

The surviving embroideries which played such an important part in the Ottoman palaces and in Ottoman society are thus of four types: embroideries made in the Palace workshop; metropolitan embroideries, some of which were made for the Palace too, from Istanbul, Edirne and Bursa; fine embroideries from provincial centres; and popular embroideries. Important provincial centres included Aydın, ʿAyntab (Gaziantep), Bandırma, Draman (in Western Thrace), Edremit, Iskeçe (Xanthi in Western Thrace), Karaman, Milâs, Rhodes, Salonike, Crete, Yanya (Ioannina in Epirus), this last particularly famous for silk-embroidered veils (*peşkir*) and napkins. Among the fine specimens of these embroideries in the Topkapı Saray collections are two over-gowns or jackets (*üstlük*), one of deep-blue woollen cloth, and one of claret-coloured velvet, made for women in Western Thrace (*ills. 120, 121*) to be worn on festivals and holidays. The Topkapı Saray collection is, however, too small to give a complete picture of popular or provincial embroideries.

The couched gold embroidery work (*zerdūz*) executed by the Palace craftsmen was obviously impossible without designs. The account of Prince Gabriel Bethlen's order (see p. 160 above) suggests that the designer may have been a specialized craftsman, not necessarily an embroiderer himself, though he would have had to have an idea of the final effect, not just the individual motifs. This might suggest further that designs in the Palace were provided by the *nakkaşhane*, the studio responsible for producing books, including their illumination and binding, for the Sultans' library. Indeed, the embroidered book binding (*ill. 95*), which in its design follows Ottoman bindings of the later sixteenth century, must certainly have been commissioned by the head of the *nakkaşhane*. But though other embroideries show certain similarities to book binding or illumination (or even, to a limited extent, to Iznik tilework), the similarities are to be found much more in individual motifs than in realized designs (compare the triple-spot design, *ill. 100*), and the closest analogies, not surprisingly, are to textiles. These, it has been argued above (see p. 23) were most probably designed not by the *nakkaşhane* but by specialized textile designers closely associated with the weavers. Moreover, quite apart from the exigencies of the medium, which in embroidery would lead to changes in motifs taken from other artefacts, it is improbable that anyone would ever have wanted embroidery to seek to copy illumination exactly. It is, for example, noteworthy that embroidery on leather in the later sixteenth century, on drinking vessels or caskets (*ills. 93, 94*) is quite different from the decoration of such objects in pottery, metal or wood.

It is possible that the members of the *cemāʿat-i zerdūzān* owed their status as paid employees of the Palace to the fact that they executed the designs for their work as well as the work itself. Alternatively, the Hungarian Ḳāsim (see p. 160 above), whose daily wage was so much more than his colleagues', may have combined his function as head of the workshop with the designing of embroideries. But, particularly as far as embroideries outside the Palace are concerned, one should remember that fine embroidery was not an Ottoman invention. The details of costume depicted in Timurid, Akkoyunlu and Safavid painting[20] show that lavishly embroidered collars, cuffs and hems were fashionable at the courts of the Ottomans' predecessors or rivals in the fifteenth and early sixteenth centuries.

And specimens of embroidery and quilting from Egypt show that it was also fashionable at the Mamlūk court in the fourteenth and fifteenth centuries.[21]

The Ottomans drew, however, on other traditions, notably those of the Mediterranean cultures and Eastern European countries which are still famous for their folk embroideries. Though the origins and development of such traditions are difficult to trace and the products tend to eclecticism, their history is undoubtedly ancient. With the rise of cheap printed pattern-books in sixteenth-century Europe, moreover, came a tremendous diffusion of patterns for embroidery and lace. Some of the earliest of these were compiled by the Venetian engraver and printer, Mathio Pagan or Pagani (fl. 1530–59), whose model-books went through numerous editions, legitimate and pirated, all over Europe, within a few years of their appearance. He was followed by many imitators, in Venice, Rome, Paris, Turin, Montbéliard, Strasbourg, Basle and Nuremberg.[22] It must be admitted that most of the designs are for lace (which, strangely, appears to be absent from Ottoman Turkey); and it is difficult to determine which similarities are significant, and which are imposed by design or technique. Nevertheless, designs in counted stitchwork or drawn-thread work in Ottoman Turkey in the sixteenth century are remarkably similar in appearance to illustrations in Pagan's pattern-books (cf. *ills. 88, 90*). These, moreover, must have been in circulation in Istanbul within a few years of their appearance, at least among the large colonies of Venetians, Florentines and Genoese resident in Galata, across the Golden Horn.

The earliest surviving sixteenth-century couched gold embroideries from the Palace workshops are from the reign of Süleymān the Magnificent (1520–66): these rare pieces are of the greatest historical interest and deserve detailed consideration. They are two splendid kaftans made for Süleymān's favourite son, Şehzāde Meḥmed, who died in 1543 at the age of 21. Both are of crimson satin. The first (*ill. 86*) is lavishly trimmed at the collar, down the front, at the hems and on the sleeves with couched gold embroidery, in bands 23 cm or more wide. Chinoiserie cloud-scrolls, a favourite sixteenth-century Ottoman motif, curved stems, florets and split-palmettes (*rūmī*), are stitched in blue silk, the cloud-scrolls being boldly modelled in navy blue. The ground is of gold thread, minutely worked and leaving no blank areas. The centres of the florets are in faded pink. The embroidery of the second kaftan (*ill. 87*) is technically similar, though the bands are narrower (14 cm wide). The design employs a motif possibly of Far Eastern origin, which appears widely in sixteenth-century Ottoman art, the so-called *chin-tamani*, a triple flaming pearl of Buddhist origin, with a pair of horizontal wavy lines, which here are treated almost as if they were antlers: the motif was adopted by the Ottomans as leopard-spots and tiger-stripes, which are attributes of the costumes of the legendary Iranian hero, Rustam. They are in bright blue on a ground of dense couched gold embroidery. The borders are of lobed palmettes and more triple spots.

The handkerchiefs (*mendīl*) from the tomb of Şehzade Meḥmed, now in the Topkapı Saray (*ill. 88*), are contemporary but in a markedly different technique. They are of fine muslin, tawny, dull-green or black, and on account of their sombre colours they are known as 'mourning' or as 'snuff' handkerchiefs. Their borders are worked in counted thread and drawn thread technique. One border is of flowers in vases in pastel tones alternating with medallions, and though the group also uses motifs drawn from Kufic script, the majority of the border designs are geometric. Another group of handkerchiefs with a known attribution is from the tomb of the famous Roxelane (Hürrem Sulṭān), the consort of Süleymān the Magnificent and a person of great influence in her time (she died in 1561). These handkerchiefs, which must have belonged to her, are some of the most elegant embroideries in the Topkapı Saray. They are of white muslin, with embroidered borders 5 cm deep (*ill. 90*). Among other embroideries from her tomb which most probably were hers is a head-band (*kasbastı*) worn to keep her head-dress in place (*ill. 89*), worked in the same technique as the handkerchief borders. There are other unattributed head-bands of the same period in the Topkapı Saray collections. There is also a group of heavily embroidered handkerchiefs which may well have been carried by Sultans on ceremonial occasions. They make lavish use of gold thread, and the borders are so deep as almost to leave no space at the middle (*ill. 91*).

Among these sixteenth-century embroideries quivers and bow-cases have an important place, and some of the finest of these are in the Topkapı Saray. These also must have been made to designs from the Palace workshop, for they were carried by the Sultans and their favourites on State occasions. They are mostly worked in couched gold thread, sometimes in relief over cotton padding, with medallions as used on book bindings and other media or with naturalistic flowers. Some are enriched with precious stones (*ill. 92*).

One of the most noteworthy Ottoman embroideries of the later sixteenth century is a book binding. It was made for a copy of Gelibolulu Muṣṭafā ʿAlī's *Nüṣret-nāme*, a chronicle of Lālā Muṣṭafā Paşa's campaigns in Georgia, Azerbaijan and Shirvan covering the years 1578–80, which was copied and illustrated in 992/1584–5 for presentation to Murād III. The binding (*ill. 95*) is of crimson silk, worked in coloured silks, gold thread and couched gold embroidery (*zerdūz*) with a central medallion, corner-pieces and a border. The medallions and corner-pieces have chinoiserie cloud-scrolls, arabesques, hyacinths, small rosettes and highly stylized chinoiserie lotus and peony in bright-blue, green and crimson silk on gold embroidery. The ground is of scrolls, florets and chinoiserie cloud-scrolls, all worked in gold thread. On the spine is the favourite sixteenth-century Ottoman motif, the leopard-spots and tiger-stripes. This binding may be used to date a drinking vessel (*maşrapa*) and an embroidered box also in the Topkapı Saray collection (*ills. 93, 94*). These are of black leather, as fine as fabric, worked with scrolling designs of cloud-scrolls and fantastically stylized chinoiserie lotus and peony, mostly in bright-blue and mauve silks but with some gold thread. Though the design of the embroidery of the box betrays the stiffness of some Venetian arabesque compositions, the similarities of workmanship show that these two pieces and the 992/1584–5 binding must be contemporary and, most probably, the work of a single craftsman. Such embroideries demonstrate the great variety of techniques that were employed at this time and the sumptuous effects achieved.

Few of the embroidered mats (*nihāli*), like the leopard-skin and Italian velvet mat listed in the 1505 inventory of the Treasury of Bāyazīd II (see p. 159 above), have survived. The Topkapı Saray collections contain, however, a remarkable rectangular crimson velvet (not illustrated), datable to the late sixteenth or early seventeenth century, embroidered all over with coloured silks and gold thread in a design somewhat similar to contemporary Uşak carpets made for the Palace. Like them, it has a central medallion and a quarter medallion at each corner. The main ground is worked with stylized carnations, tulips, foliage and chinoiserie cloud-scrolls. The borders are of green velvet worked with flowers.[23] Another remarkable piece, which is unpublished, is a fine round leather *nihāli* in the library of the castle of Skokloster outside Stockholm, combining embroidery with cut-out work and appliqué. Skokloster was built by Carl Gustav Wrangel (1613–76), Marshal of Sweden for the latter part of his life. He spent much of his career on campaigns in Germany and Eastern Europe, and indeed sacked Prague in 1648, when he may well have acquired the *nihāli* as booty from the collection of Rudolf II. But he was a great collector too and may have bought it as a curiosity. Alternatively, it may have been acquired by his grandson at the Battle of Mohács in 1687, along with a Turkish tent which he brought back as booty to Skokloster.

As for Ottoman embroideries of this sixteenth-century classical period executed by women in the Harem or outside the Palace, these also use both gold thread and coloured silks, but on light materials like fine linen or muslin, for wrappers, veils and various small cloths. The surviving pieces from this period may be divided into two categories. One group is more loosely worked, on fine soft linen, with motifs somewhat reminiscent of contemporary Iznik tilework. The women may have worked from sketches, or may have created new compositions based on assorted motifs from tilework, textiles or carpets, using pomegranate flowers or fruit, artichokes or cardoons, cloud-scrolls and various sorts of florists' flowers on a white or cream ground. The principal colours are crimson and blue, though black, bright green and even yellow are used. The use of black for outlines, moreover, may indicate attention to Iznik tilework where motifs are characteristically outlined in darker colours, though it is often difficult to tell because the black dye had a tendency to rot the silk fibres and has often disappeared. A noteworthy specimen of this group is a wrapper (*bohça*) with a contemporary label stating that it belonged to a certain Gevher Sulṭān (*ill. 96*). The design is of overall repeating motifs of spiky stylized lotuses enclosed by pairs of serrated leaves, reminiscent of Bursa medallion silks. The Gevher Sulṭān to whom the wrapper belonged is very probably to be identified with the lady of that name who was a daughter of Selīm II (1566–74), which could date it to the last quarter of the sixteenth century. These designs established a tradition, however, and continue well into the seventeenth century.

A second group is distinguished by its delicacy of design and fine workmanship. The pieces are typically turban-covers which were employed to protect the turbans of Ottoman notables when not in use (when they were not being worn turbans were placed on special stands or *kavukluk*) and keep them clean. There is a fine turban-cover (*ill. 98*) with richly varied floral motifs and featuring an elaborate colour-scheme that suggests that this example may have been made for a Sultan, or at least from a design drawn by the Palace embroidery workshop. It shows a bouquet in a vase of a cypress tree, artichokes, carnations and tulips. On the borders the same florists' flowers appear side by side, as in a herbaceous border, or entwined with one another. The piece is datable to the late sixteenth or early seventeenth century.

One of the choicest specimens of seventeenth-century Palace embroidery is a prayer mat (*seccāde*) of fine crimson moiré silk (*ill. 102*), which must have been made either for a Sultan or for an important member of his suite. The design is a three-arched mihrab on two slender columns with a mosque lamp hanging in each arch. Below, the place to stand is indicated by a pair of footprints with date palms and tulips. The spandrels contain similar stylized palm trees and cloud-bands. The green silk borders have repeating trees. This is the earliest datable prayer mat in the Topkapı Saray collections and seems to have been one of a pair. It owes its excellent state of preservation to the fact that it has scarcely been used.

Important Palace embroideries in the seventeenth century were still worked in gold thread. There are extant pieces of prime quality in several European collections. Since some of these are more or less precisely datable, they may be used as a basis for dating other pieces. One such is an embroidered saddle-cloth sent in 1626 from Istanbul as a gift to Gustavus Adolphus of Sweden, who was a relation by marriage of George I Rákóczy, Prince of Transylvania (cf. p. 160 above). It is of crimson velvet worked in gold thread with a design of stylized foliate motifs, including pomegranates filled with small bunches or sprigs of flowers. The Topkapı Saray collection contains several pieces that are similar, in technique or decoration, in particular, a crimson velvet bag for a banner (*ill. 101*) worked with wrapped gold thread in high relief, with stylized pomegranates. Embroideries in this technique continue into the second half of the seventeenth century.

By far the largest group of surviving embroideries is from the eighteenth and nineteenth centuries. They make wide use of techniques and materials and reflect the changes in taste resulting from increasing European influence on the arts of Ottoman Turkey, notably in the growing taste for 'Western' perspective landscape wall-painting. This shows itself in embroideries in the decoration of napkins, bath-towels, bolster-covers and even tent borders, with embroidered scenes of rivers, bridges, trees or ships (cf. *ill. 118*). Western influence also shows itself in changes in the fashionable colours. The taste for predominantly crimson and blue embroideries that prevailed in the sixteenth and seventeenth centuries gave way to pastel colours. A cloth of embroidered cream satin (*ill. 105*) is very typical of the change. Designed to go under trays of food, it is worked in various pastel tones and silver thread with embossed naturalistic flowers springing from vases. The motifs chosen and their arrangement also demonstrate the influence of Western European taste at the Ottoman Court.

A favourite technique of the eighteenth and nineteenth centuries was needlework (*sûzenî*) on cloth tautened on an embroidery frame: later such work was done by machine. From the sources we may infer that the technique was also practised earlier, in the preceding two centuries, though practically nothing of it has survived. The Topkapı Saray collections contain many late pieces. One of these is a prayer rug (*ill. 106, detail*) datable to the late eighteenth century, worked on heavy crimson wool and featuring a mihrab, with heavy flowers and foliage in the spandrels and at the sides and a hanging mosque lamp. The borders have a repeating floral scroll. Another fine piece of *sûzenî* work is a barber's towel (*önlük*) of pale-green silk with buds and sprigged blossoms in silver thread and blue and lilac silks (*ill. 107*). Sprigged flowers or bunches or blossoms were much favoured for the decoration of later Turkish embroideries, particularly for the materials used for women's or children's dresses (cf. *ill. 39*). Materials for these were embroidered first and tailored afterwards, and in the Topkapı Saray there are lengths of cloth, embroidered with spangles and metal thread, which have never been made up into garments (*ill. 113*).

As in earlier periods, embroideries worked with gold thread remain important. Possibly under Westernizing influence embroidery in metal thread was normally in the wrapped thread technique. A fine example of this is a round leather case for a coffee-pot on which the pot itself was placed, tied up and kept hot while being brought from the kitchen to wherever it was to be served (*ill. 109*). Embroidery in gold and coloured silks on an embossed foundation, known as *dıval*-work, was much practised in the eighteenth and nineteenth centuries and fine pieces were made both inside and outside the Palace in Istanbul and in provincial centres like Maraş and Trabzon. In this technique, which is one of considerable antiquity,[24] designs were cut out in pasteboard or thin leather, were tacked on to the material and were then entirely sewn over with gold or silver thread. A masterpiece in this laborious technique in the Topkapı Saray is another prayer mat, this time of purple silk (*ill. 112*). The upper part is worked with foliate arabesques (*rūmī*) and flowers in silver thread. The mihrab is of beige velvet worked in similar technique with similar scroll-work. Another piece of *dıval*-work is a mauve satin bedspread (*ill. 110*), with embroidery also in wrapped thread technique, with a central medallion, corner decoration and borders of foliate scroll and flowers. The materials and technique are traditional enough, but the motifs show Western influence.

Various jewelled, pearled or metal-thread embroideries from the Palace workshop of this late period have also survived – sashes, garments, wrappers, wall-hangings, prayer mats and round mats for the service of coffee. Documents in the Topkapı Saray Archives give further information on the widespread use of embroidered cloths in the nineteenth century; one example is an account of the furnishings of the room in which Ṣāliḥa Sulṭān, the daughter of Maḥmūd II (1808–39), was born. For her mother's bed were brought out sheets and quilts with pearls, precious stones and gold-thread embroidery, and there were similar cloths for the baby's cradle. The divan, the cushions and the bolsters of the birth chamber were of pink cloth of gold embroidered with spangles. The floor-coverings and the door- and window-curtains were of similar material similarly embroidered. In all there were 60 cloths, all heavily embroidered with metal thread, sequins and pearls. Unfortunately, none of these has survived. Of comparable quality, however, is a rectangular cloth (*ill. 114*) worked with metal thread and pearls. At the centre is a sunburst medallion, with quarter medallions at the corners. The borders have heraldic compositions of musical instruments and trophies alternating with floral garlands. Among other embroideries with pearls and metal-thread coffee-cloths are prominent: they were used when coffee was served ceremonially by the *kahvecibaşı* and are particularly sumptuous. The Topkapı Saray collection contains pieces thickly embroidered with yellow metal thread and pearls (*ills. 115, 116*). And in the Hazine (the Treasury section) there is exhibited a metal-embroidered coffee-cloth with a diamond rosette at the centre.

These late embroideries show that the impulse to the luxurious and extravagant decoration of textiles, which is such a mark of the Sultans' courts in the sixteenth and seventeenth centuries, did not slacken and only lapsed with the fall of the Ottoman Empire. At the present time attempts are being made to revive, in technical institutes and craft schools, the techniques and motifs of this great and long-lived school.

Notes to Historical Documentation

1 C. White, *Three years in Constantinople, or Domestic manners of the Turks in 1844*, 3 vols. (London 1845) I, 193, 214.

2 Ömer Lûtfi Barkan, *Süleymaniye Camii ve Imareti Inşatı* II (Ankara 1979), 281, no. 577, I. 24. The list forms part of the building accounts for the mosque of Sultan Aḥmed in Istanbul. Furnishings of this type might have been a standard item in such accounts, but no other lists have yet come to light.

3 J. M. Rogers, 'An Ottoman palace inventory of the reign of Bayazid II', *VIe Colloque du CIEPO, Cambridge 1984*, ed. J.-L. Bacqué-Grammont (Istanbul 1986). The inventory is reproduced in *Topkapı Sarayı Müzesi Arşiv Kılavuzu* (Istanbul 1938).

4 Topkapı Saray Archives, D.9613–1. The section on the embroiderers does not appear to have been published. Cf. Rıfkı Melûl Meriç, *Türk Nakış Sanatı Tarihi Araştırmaları I. Vesikalar* (Ankara 1953), v–viii.

5 R. Lopez, 'Silk industry in the Byzantine Empire', *Speculum* XX (1945), 1–42, *ad* note 28.

6 Rıfkı Melûl Meriç, 'Bayramlarda Padişahlara hediye edilen san'at eserleri ve karşılıkları', *Türk San'atı Tarihi Araştırma ve Incemeleri* I (1963), 764–86.

7 Ahmet Refik, *Hicrî on ikinci asırda Istanbul Hayatı (1100–1200)* (Istanbul 1930), no. 79.

8 Veronika Gervers, *The influence of Ottoman Turkish textiles and costume in Eastern Europe* (Royal Ontario Museum, Toronto 1982), 6–9.

9 B. Radvánsky, *Udvartartások és számadáskönyvek. I. Bethlen Gabor fejedelem udvartarása* (Household and account books I. The household of Prince Gabriel Bethlen) (Budapest 1888), 157.

10 Dated 1632, A. Beke and S. Barabás, *I. Rákóczy György és a Porta. Levelek és okiratok* (George Rákóczy and the Porte. Letters and documents) (Budapest 1880), 45.

11 *The six voyages of John Baptiste Tavernier, Baron of Aubonne*, made English by J.P. (London 1677), 38.

12 Topkapı Saray Archives, D.12a–b.

13 M. S. Kütükoğlu, *Osmanlılarda narh müessesesi ve 1640 tarihli narh defteri* (Istanbul 1983).

14 Marino Sanuto, *Diarii* XLIX (1897), 182.

15 J. von Hammer-Purgstall, *Geschichte des Osmanischen Reiches* VIII (Pest 1832), 481–7.

16 V. Gervers, op. cit., 6–9, 36–7.

17 Lady Mary Wortley Montagu to the Countess of Mar, Adrianople, 1 April 1717 (O.S.).

18 *Türkische Kunst und Kultur aus Osmanischer Zeit*, 4/14 and Pl. IX.

19 Lady Mary Wortley Montagu to the Countess of Mar, Adrianople, 18 April 1717 (O.S.).

20 E.g., in Topkapı Saray Library, album H.2153.

21 Wafiyya ʿIzzī, 'Objects bearing the name of an-Nāṣir and his successors', in *Colloque International sur l'Histoire du Caire*, ed. A. Raymond, M. Rogers and M. Wahba (Leipzig–Cairo 1973), 235–41; also C. J. Lamm, 'Some Mamlūk embroideries', *Ars Islamica* IV (1937), 65–76.

22 For example, Mathio Pagan, *La Gloria et l'Honore de ponti tagliati, e ponti in aere* (Venetia, Mathio Pagan, 1558; facsimile London, 1884). See also M. Dreger, *Entwicklungsgeschichte der Spitze* (Vienna 1902), and A. Lodz, *Bibliographie der Modellbücher* (Leipzig 1933).

23 *The Anatolian Civilisations*, E 141; W. Denny in Y. Petsopoulos (ed.), *Tulips, Arabesques and Turbans* (London 1981), No. 130.

24 Richard Ettinghausen, 'Foundation-moulded leatherwork – a rare Egyptian technique also used in Britain', in *Studies in Islamic Art and Architecture in honour of Professor K. A. C. Creswell*, (AUC Press, Cairo 1965), 63–71.

CAPTIONS AND NOTES TO ILLUSTRATIONS 86–121

86 Detail of the embroidery (hems, cuffs and facing) of the crimson kaftan of Şehzāde Meḥmed (d. 1543), son of Süleymān the Magnificent, couched gold thread (*zerdūz*), with cloud-bands and floral scrolls in deep red, black, pale-blue and faded-pink silk, Palace workshop, *c.* 1540; 35/1147. Length 149 cm, width of embroidered facing 21 cm.
□ Örcün Barışta, *Osmanlı imperatorluk dönemi Türk işlemelerinden örnekler*, 121, No. 68 (giving the old number 13/739); *The Anatolian Civilisations*, E 101; *Türkische Kunst und Kultur aus osmanischer Zeit*, 5/4.

87 Detail of a kaftan of Şehzāde Meḥmed, son of Süleymān the Magnificent, striped crimson satin with white damask and silver braid on the breast, with embroidered facings in couched gold thread (*zerdūz*) and lobed panels, florets, triple spots and tiger-stripes in black, bright-blue, deep-red and faded-pink silks, Palace workshops, *c.* 1540; 35/1144. Length 143 cm.
□ Barışta, op. cit., No. 2 (giving old number 13/738); Macide Gönül, *Turkish embroideries XVI-XIX centuries* (Istanbul n.d.), Plate 31; Walter Denny, 'Textiles' in Yanni Petsopoulos (ed.), *Tulips, Arabesques and Turbans* (London 1981), No. 135; Esin Atıl (ed.), *Turkish Art*, 335, Plate 64.

88 Details of handkerchiefs thought to have belonged to Şehzade Meḥmed (died October 1543), from the tomb of Şehzade Meḥmed at Şehzadebaşı, Istanbul, fine muslin, the borders worked with coloured silks enhanced with metal thread, Palace workshop, *c.* 1540; 31/53, 54, 59, 60. Each 52 cm square.
The designs are partly printed in black on the muslin and partly openwork.
□ *The Anatolian Civilisations*, E 97, E 99 and cf. E 98 (from the same tomb). Cf. Barışta, Nos. 8, 11–13; Gönül, Pl. 18.

89 Lady's head-band (*kasbastı*), used to keep the head-dress in position, from the tomb of Roxelane (Hürrem Sulṭān) at Süleymaniye, linen, embroidered in counted stitch work with coloured silks and gold and silver thread, Palace workshop, *c.* 1561; 31/1479. 4 × 53 cm.
For another head-band also associated with Hürrem Sultan, cf. *The Anatolian Civilisations*, E 100.
□ Barışta, No. 15; Gönül, Pl. 17a–c; *Türkische Kunst und Kultur aus osmanischer Zeit*, 5/7.

90 Handkerchief, from the tomb of Roxelane (Hürrem Sulṭān) at Süleymaniye, pinkish cream muslim with embroidered borders in coloured silks and gold thread, Palace workshop, *c.* 1561; 31/1473. 46 cm square.
□ Barışta, No. 6; and cf. Gönül, Pl. 20.

91 Ceremonial or dress handkerchief, linen, with borders and a central medallion heavily embroidered in gold thread and black, crimson and green silks with cloud-bands and floral motifs, Palace workshop, mid-sixteenth century; 31/1484. 65 cm square; width of border 18 cm.
□ Cf. Barışta, No. 9 (31/1484).

92 Bow-case, covered with crimson velvet, embroidered in gold thread and coloured silks with arabesque medallions and triple spots treated as crescents, Palace workshops, mid-sixteenth century; 1/1989. 72 × 30 cm.
□ Gönül, Pl. 22.

93 Mug, black leather, embroidered in relief in gold thread and coloured silks, with chinoiserie floral scroll, Palace workshop, late sixteenth century; 31/276. Height 14 cm.
The embroidery technique is similar to that seen in ill. 94. There is a *tombak* (gilt copper) mug of comparable shape and date in the Walters Art Gallery, Baltimore, Md (54.512). The shape, however, is most characteristic of leatherwork and is closely related to South German *Humpen* forms of the later Middle Ages.

94 Box, black leather on a wood frame, fastenings and armature gold, embroidered in couched gold thread (*zerdūz*) in strap stitch, stem stitch and gold thread in relief on successive layers of coloured silks, with a dense foliate scroll, a bold cruciform medallion and chinoiserie peony and lotus, Palace workshop, *c.* 1584; 31/268. 16 × 27 × 14 cm.
□ *The Anatolian Civilisations*, E 117.

continued on page 209

Opposite
Detail of illustration 114

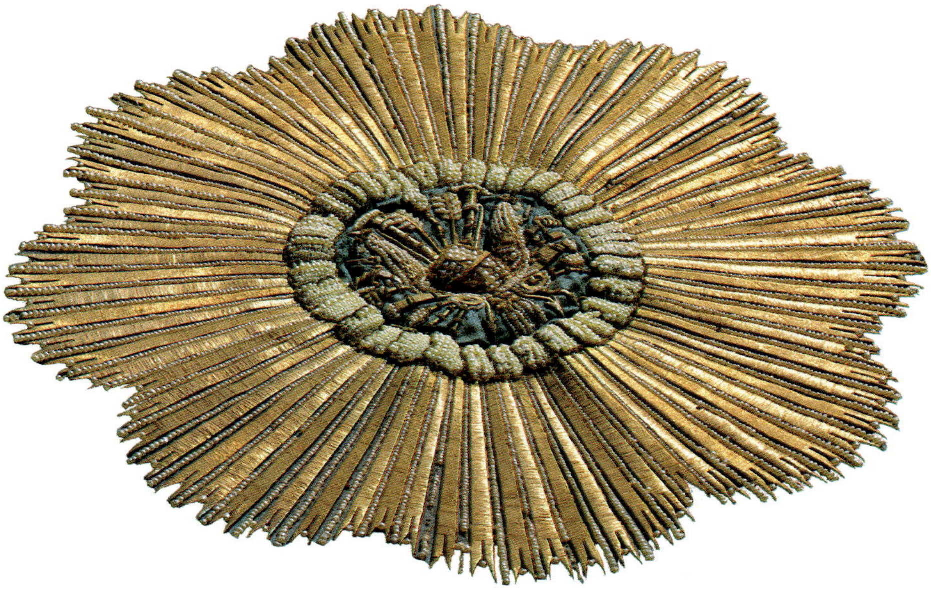

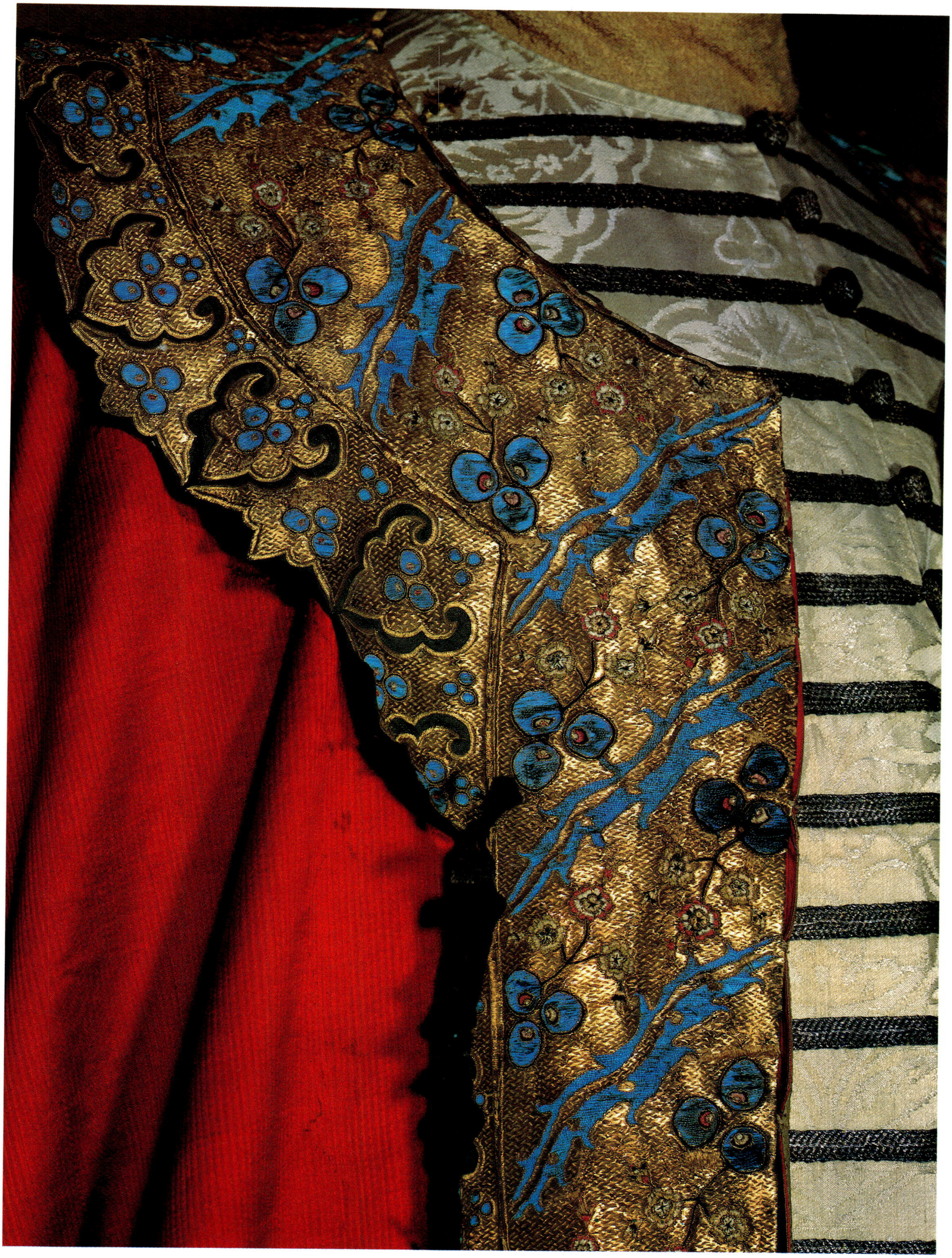

88

89

90

91

94

96

97

103

104

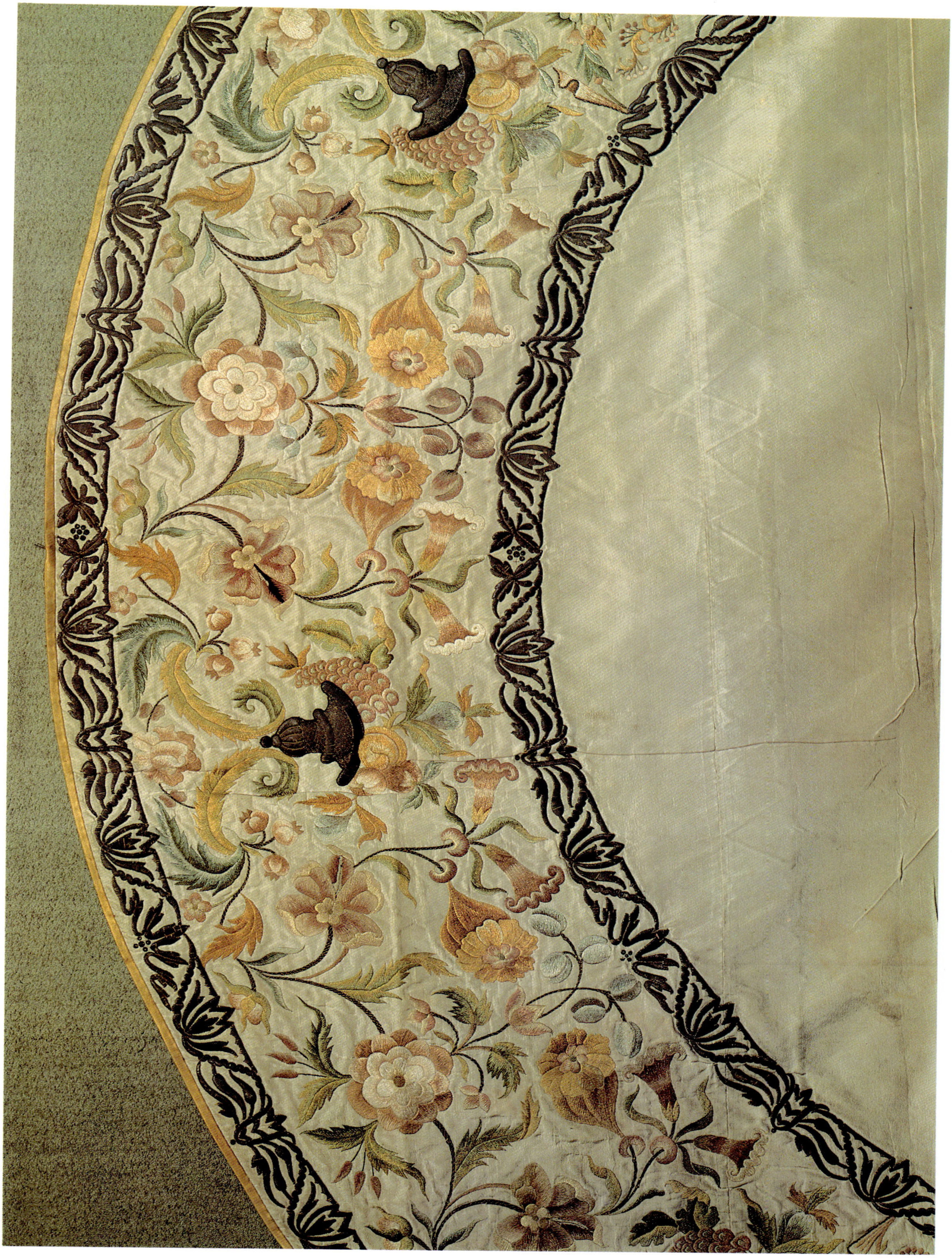

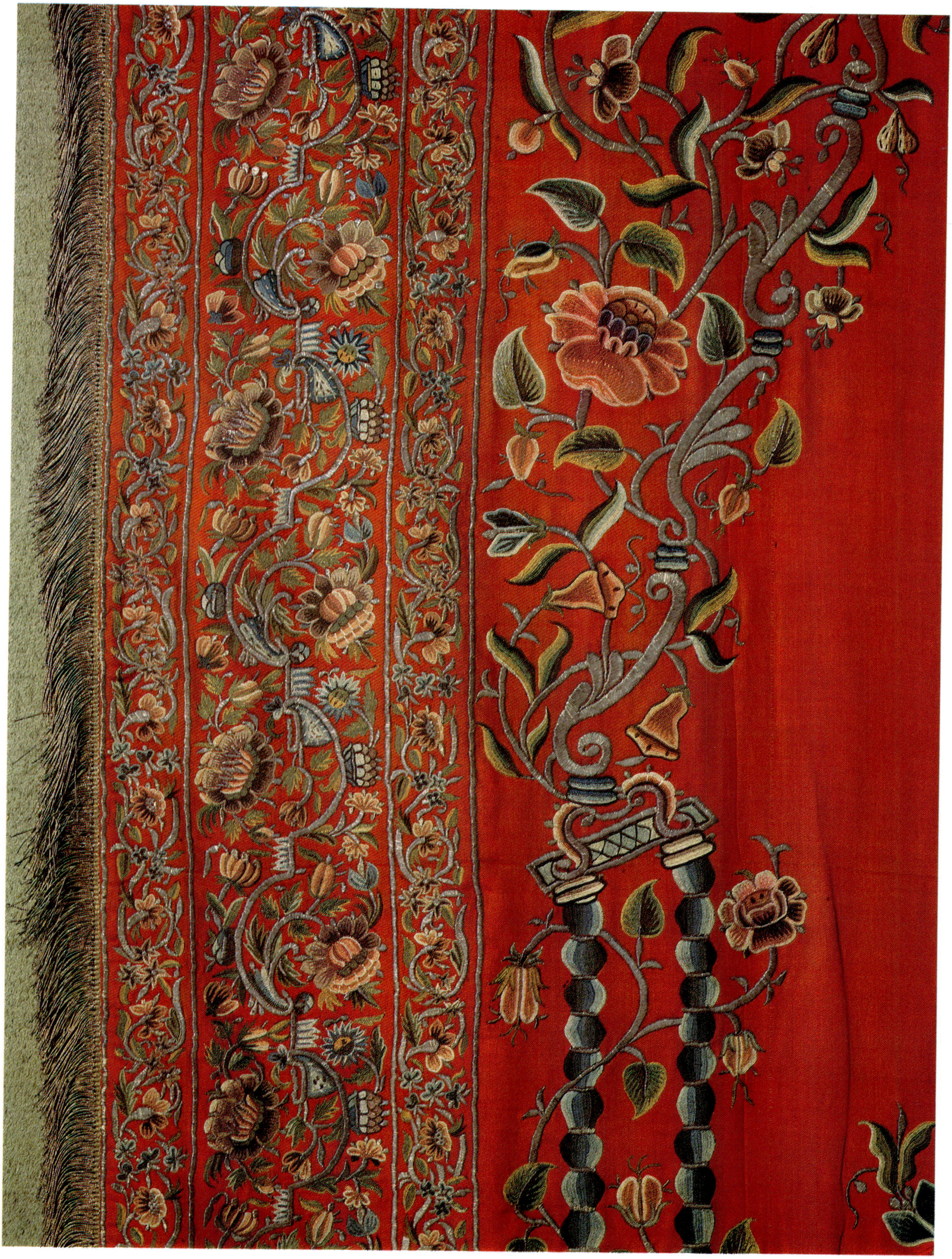

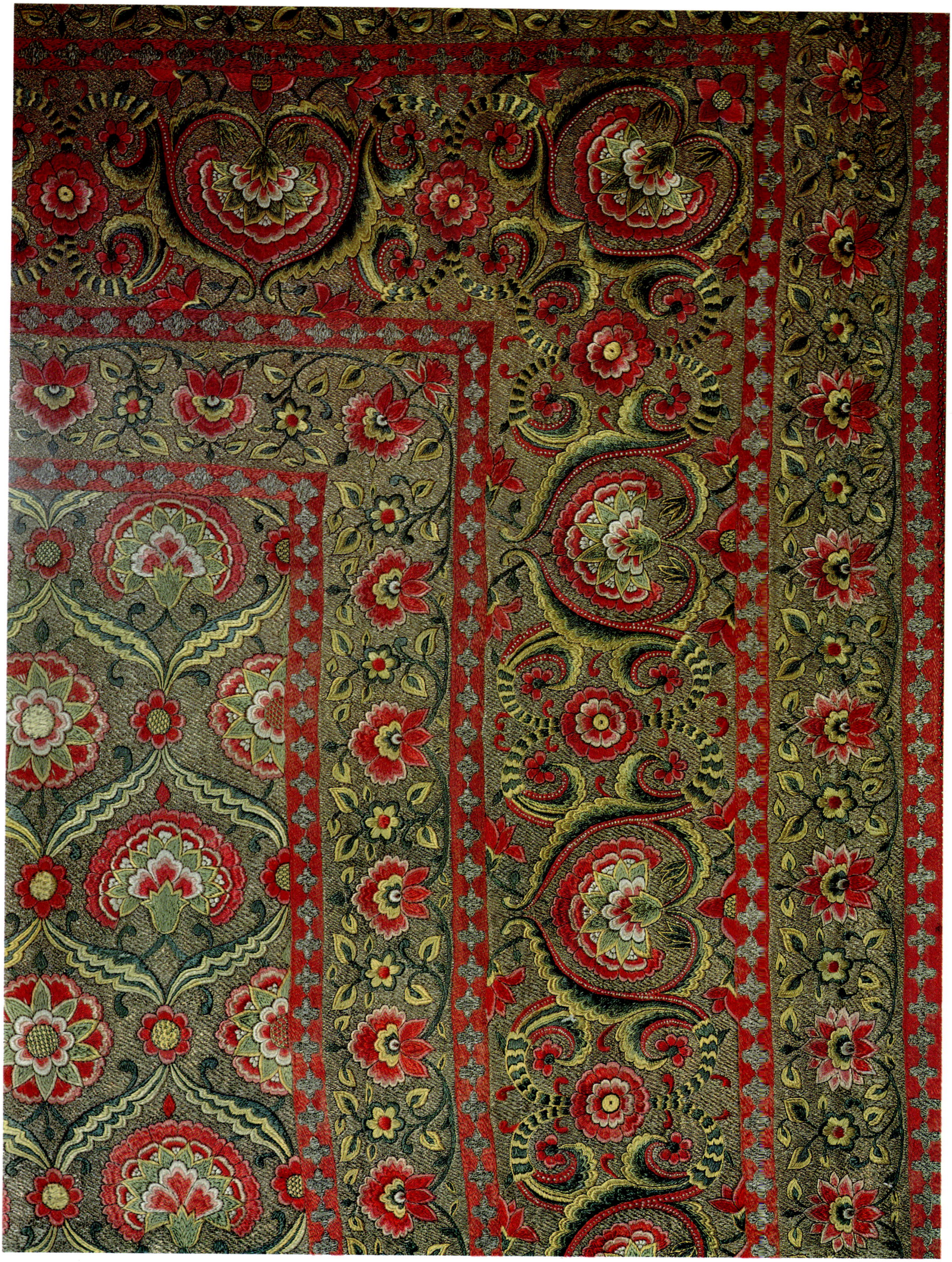

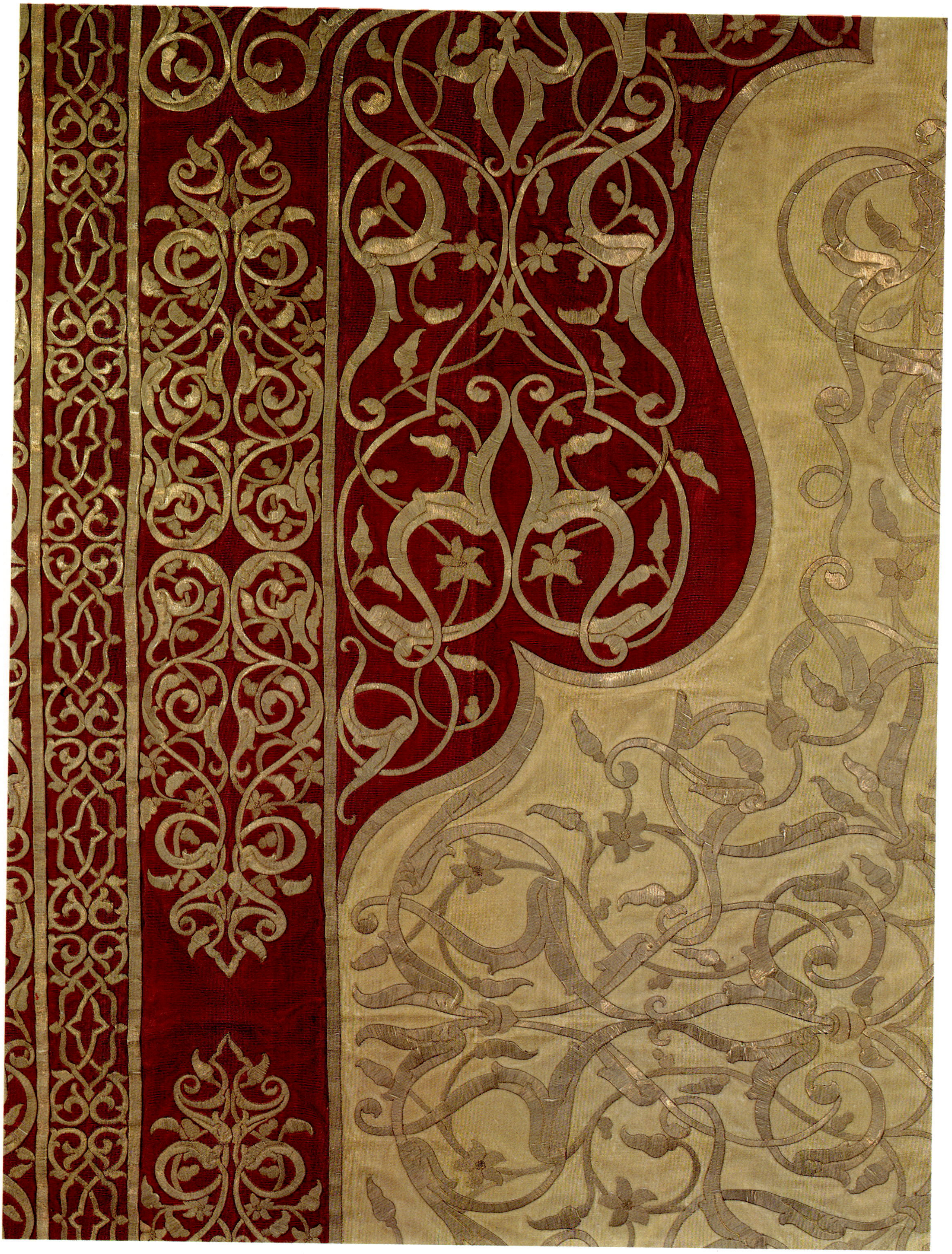

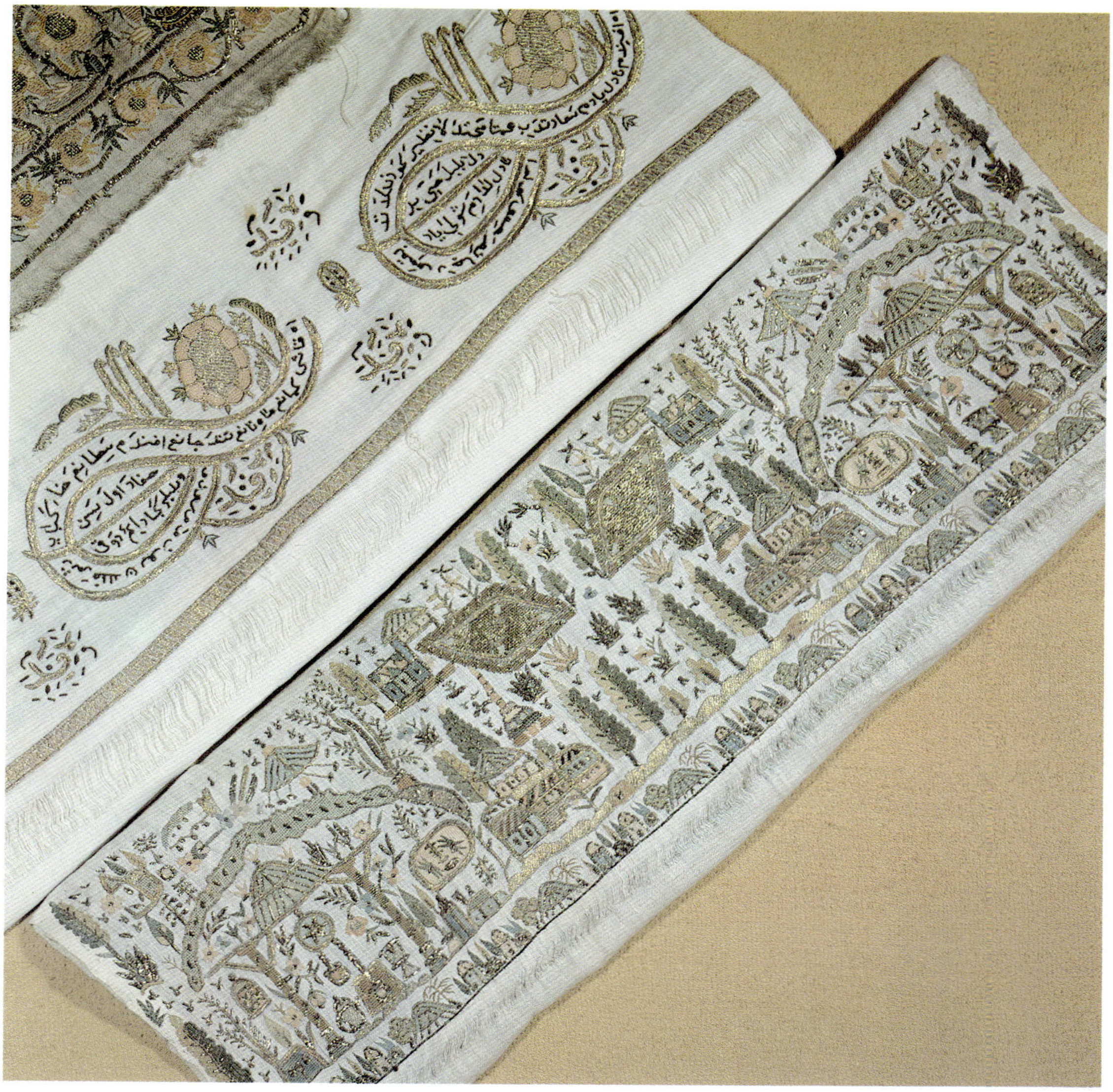

118

119

CAPTIONS AND NOTES TO ILLUSTRATIONS

continued from page 168

95 *Nüṣretnāme* of Gelibolulu Muṣṭafā ʿAlī, copied 992/1584–5, leather binding, embroidered in gold in satin stitch, double darning and stem stitch with cloud-bands, flowers and triple spots, with leopard-spots and tiger-stripes on the spine, Palace workshop, late sixteenth century; Topkapı Saray Library, H.1365, 38·5 × 23 cm.
For another embroidered leather binding of the same period, cf. Topkapı Saray Library, A.6570 (*The Anatolian Civilisations*, E 181).
☐ *The Anatolian Civilisations*, E 124.

96 Detail of wrapper (*bohça*), beige linen, embroidered with multicoloured silks in double darning stitch (*pesent*) with stylized heart-shaped lotus medallions enclosed by feathery leaves, associated with Gevher Sultan (died 1574), a daughter of Selīm II, Palace workshop, 1575–1600; 31/15. 106 × 102 cm.
The design appears to derive from a Bursa brocade, cf. a velvet in the Topkapı Saray, early seventeenth century, 13/1450 (*The Anatolian Civilisations*, E 246).
☐ *The Anatolian Civilisations*, E 245; Gönül, Pl. 6.

97 Bedspread (detail), fine linen worked with coloured silks with stylized tulips, roses and other floral motifs, Palace workshop, early seventeenth century; 31/1183. 245 × 135 cm.

98 Turban-cover (detail), cream compound silk-cotton cloth, embroidered in coloured silks with somewhat stylized hyacinths, tulips, carnations and pomegranates, Palace workshop, late sixteenth or early seventeenth century; 31/67. 198 × 121 cm.
The turban-cover is from the tomb of Şehzāde Meḥmed (died October 1543) at Şehzadebaşı in Istanbul, but was evidently placed on his cenotaph at some later date.
☐ Barışta, No. 56, and compare Nos. 54–5; Gönül, Pl. 10.

99 Napkin (detail), fine linen, worked in coloured silks with sprays of flowers and leaves drawn in black, late seventeenth or early eighteenth century; 31/1199. 125 × 23 cm.
☐ Barışta, No. 82; cf. Gönül, Pl. 26.

100 Detail of wrapper (*bohça*), yellow satin, worked in coloured silks with repeating triple-spot or crescent motifs framed by serrated leaves, all outlined in black which in places has fallen away, seventeenth century; 31/7, 124 × 30 cm.
For a turban-cover with triple-spot embroidery, cf. Barışta, No. 29 (Topkapı Saray, 31/71).
☐ Walter Denny in Y. Petsopoulos (ed.), op. cit., No. 148; Gönül, Pl. 12.

101 Bag for a banner, crimson velvet, embroidered with silver thread on a yellow silk core (giving the appearance of gold) and coloured silks with stylized pomegranate motifs, Palace workshop, seventeenth century; 31/170. 124 × 26 cm.
☐ Barışta, No. 42.

102 Prayer mat (*seccāde*), heavy crimson silk worked in coloured silks with a triple-niched mihrab, with stylized tulip and palm-tree finials, cloud-bands in the spandrels, openwork mosque lamps, and the place for the feet indicated; the border is of dark-green moiré, worked with repeating stylized palm trees. Palace workshop, seventeenth century; 31/9. 192 × 130 cm.
There is a similar prayer mat, of similar date, with a single-arched mihrab on crimson and green moiré, in the Topkapı Saray, 31/1359 (cf. Barışta, No. 63).
☐ Barışta, No. 64; *The Anatolian Civilisations*, E 238.

103 Wrapper (detail), deep-mauve satin, worked with sprigged flowers, birds and scrolls in coloured silks and metal thread, eighteenth century; 31/1163. 98 cm square.

104 Wrapper (detail), crimson satin, with a border of yellow satin and corner-pieces of blue, worked in contrasting coloured silks with whirling rosettes, eighteenth century; 31/6. 124 × 130 cm.
☐ Walter Denny in Y. Petsopoulos (ed.), op. cit., No. 149; Gönül, Pl. 14.

105 Tablecloth (detail), cream satin, embroidered in silver and gold thread and coloured silks with a border of cornucopias and scrolls with heavy flowers and leaves partly deriving from the repertory of bizarre silks from Lyons, Palace workshop, eighteenth–nineteenth century; 31/28. Diameter 190 cm.
☐ Barışta, No. 161.

106 Prayer mat (detail) crimson wool (*lahuraki*) with heavy needlework (*sûzenî*) in metal thread and coloured silks, the mihrab spandrels being filled with arabesques and the scrolling borders with flowers deriving from the repertory of chintzes, Palace workshop, eighteenth century; 31/514. 185 × 105 cm.

107 Barber's towel (*önlük*), pale greenish silk, worked in silver thread and coloured silks with sprigged blossoms and a border of heavier flowers and stylized pomegranates at the collar, late eighteenth or early nineteenth century; 31/1084. 150 × 100 cm.
☐ Barışta, No. 195.

108 Detail of an embroidered mat (*nihāli*), worked in wrapped silver thread and coloured silks on a metal-thread ground with stylized carnations and fantastic flowers, Palace workshop, eighteenth century; 31/11. 257 × 114 cm.

109 Case for a coffee-pot, black leather, embroidered in metal thread with ribbands and flowering stems, some with acanthus volutes, Palace workshop, early nineteenth century; 31/251. Diameter 30 cm.

110 Bedspread (detail), deep-mauve satin, heavily embroidered with metal thread over a pasteboard foundation (*dıval*), with radial scrolling sprays and fat fantastic blooms, Palace workshop, late eighteenth or early nineteenth century; 31/1849. 215 × 175 cm.
□ Barışta, No. 199.

111 Bolster-case (detail), heavy silk cloth embroidered with metal thread over a pasteboard foundation, with radial scrolling stems of Convolvulus or Ipomaea flowers, nineteenth century; 31/963. 125 cm square.

112 Prayer mat (detail), the field beige silk and the spandrels of the mihrab deep purple, heavily embroidered in gold thread over a pasteboard foundation with foliate arabesques (*rūmī*), buds and flowers, Palace workshops, nineteenth century or later; 31/1808. 192 × 130 cm.
□ *The Anatolian Civilisations*, E 342; Barışta, No. 190.

113 Bright-red woollen cloth, embroidered in gold thread and spangles with a repeating design of undulating leafy stems and floral sprays, Palace workshop, nineteenth century; 31/228. 600 × 57 cm.

114 Tablecloth (detail), bright-blue satin, heavily embroidered with gold and silver thread and pearls, with musical instruments, trophies and a sunburst at the centre, Palace workshop, nineteenth century; 2/3507. 170 cm square.
□ Barışta, No. 164.

115 Cloth for a coffee service (detail), deep-violet satin, with embroidery in gold and silver thread, cording, sequins and pearls, with bouquets of stylized roses andother florists' flowers in satin stitch over a pasteboard foundation, nineteenth century; 2/5571. Diameter 93 cm.
□ Barışta, No. 155; *The Anatolian Civilisations*, E 362.

116 Cloth for a coffee service (detail), pink satin, heavily embroidered in satin stitch over a pasteboard foundation with gold and silver thread, cording and spangles with thistles and other flowers, Palace workshop, nineteenth century; 2/4656. Diameter 96 cm.
□ Barışta, No. 156.

117 Sash (detail), fine white cotton, worked in coloured silks with bunches of flowers in baskets, mid-eighteenth century; 31/1180. 260 × 34 cm.

118 Embroidered ends to two towels (*makrama*), white cotton or linen, worked with coloured silks and gold thread, eighteenth–nineteenth century; 31/1392, 31/136. Each 170 × 78 cm overall.
The upper towel is embroidered with imitation Imperial cyphers (*tuğra*) and verses; Barışta, No. 290. The lower towel bears pavilions and trees in a schematic landscape; Barışta, No. 286. Towels with similar decoration of stylized buildings by rivers are well represented in the collections of the Topkapı Saray and other museums. Cf. *The Anatolian Civilisations*, E 300 (31/1845); Barışta, Nos. 250–7 (31/1179, 31/1071, 31/1267, 31/1399).

119 Napkin, fine cream linen, embroidered in metal thread and coloured silks with stylized pomegranate motifs, blossoms and leaves, late eighteenth century; 31/312. 150 × 53 cm.

120 Detail of sleeveless Thracian woman's over-gown (*üstlük*), claret-coloured velvet, with spangles, silver cord and couched heavy gold braiding, nineteenth century; 13/2165. Length 115 cm.

121 Detail of sleeveless Thracian woman's over-gown (*üstlük*), deep-blue wool, with spangles, silver cord and braiding in metal thread, nineteenth century; 13/1594. Length 115 cm.

Bibliographical note

The following works are cited in abbreviated form in the notes on the illustrations:

The Anatolian Civilisations, exhibition catalogue (Istanbul 1983)

E. Atıl (ed.), *Turkish Art* (Washington DC–New York 1981)

Örcün Barışta, *Osmanlı imperatorluk dönemi Türk işlemelerinden örnekler* (Ankara 1981)

Raymond Cox, *Les Soieries d'art* (Paris 1914)

Ernst Flemming, *Encyclopaedia of Textiles* (2nd ed., revised by Renate Jaques, London 1958)

Macide Gönül, *Turkish embroideries XVI–XIX centuries* (Istanbul n.d.)

Tahsin Öz, *Türk Kumaş ve Kadifeleri*, 2 vols.: vol. I (Istanbul 1946) published in English as *Turkish Textiles and Velvets: XIV–XVI Centuries* (Ankara 1950); vol. II in Turkish only (Istanbul 1951)

Türkische Kunst und Kultur aus osmanischer Zeit, exhibition catalogue, Frankfurt/Main–Essen 1985)

Concordance of Topkapı Saray Museum inventory numbers and items illustrated in this volume

COSTUMES

Topkapı reference	*Illustration number*
13/6	2
13/8	1
13/9	48
13/34	4
13/35	3
13/37	18
13/38	6
13/39	11
13/40	5
13/41	10
13/42	8
13/46	7
13/99	15
13/110	13
13/111	17
13/112	16
13/176	19
13/177	20
13/195	21
13/198	26
13/199	24
13/216	23
13/221	25
13/263	37
13/265	32
13/266	33
13/267	30
13/268	34
13/269	35

Topkapı reference	*Illustration number*
13/275	36
13/277	29
13/357	40
13/360	42
13/365	39
13/408	44
13/413	46
13/470	41
13/486	22
13/489	47
13/500	49
13/512	50
13/514	51
13/522	53
13/525	52
13/532	54
13/554	57
13/557	55
13/558	56
13/584	38
13/589	59
13/595	58
13/608	73
13/623	74
13/626	75
13/631	76
13/644	78
13/689	77

Topkapı reference	*Illustration number*
13/670	79
13/699	83
13/701	84
13/715	80
13/716	81
13/731	85
13/795	72
13/803	62
13/804	64
13/805	61
13/807	60
13/808	71
13/812	66
13/814	63
13/815	65
13/816	69
13/818	68
13/819	67
13/820	70
13/830	12
13/831	9
13/834	27
13/835	28
13/837	31
13/838	45
13/839	43
13/840	14
13/848	82

EMBROIDERIES

Topkapı reference	*Illustration number*
(Library)	
H.1365	95
(Museum)	
1/1989	92
2/3507	114
2/4656	116
2/5571	115
31/6	104
31/7	100
31/9	102
31/11	108
31/15	96
31/28	105
31/53, 54, 59, 60	88
31/67	98
31/136	118
31/170	101

Topkapı reference	*Illustration number*
31/228	113
31/251	109
31/268	94
31/276	93
31/312	119
31/514	106
31/963	111
31/1084	107
31/1144	87
31/1147	86
31/1163	103
31/1180	117
31/1183	97
31/1199	99
31/1392	118
31/1473	90
31/1479	89
31/1484	91
31/1594	121
31/1808	112
31/1849	110
31/2165	120

Index

Numbers in italics refer to illustrations and/or their relevant captions and notes.

ʿAbbās I (Shah) 15
ʿAbbāsids 13, 14
ʿAbdü'l-ʿAzīz (Sultan) *84*
ʿAbdü'l-Hamīd I (Sultan) *73*
ʿAbdü'l-Mecīd (Sultan) 161, *80–2*
Adrianople, *see* Edirne
Aelst, Peter Coecke van 13
Aḥmed I (Sultan) 11, 12, *29–34*; mosque 159
Aḥmed II (Sultan) *52, 53*
Aḥmed III (Sultan) 11, 27, *54*
Aḥmed Beg (furrier) 44
Aleppo 15, 17, 32, 39
Alexandria 7, 14, 31, 32
ʿAlī (Caliph) 14
ʿAli Ağa 155 (*57*)
Anatolia 19, 34, 39; peasant dress 25
Ankara 20, 33, 40
Arte della Seta 21, 22, 23

Badr, Battle of 14
Baghdad 12, 13, 34
Banchi (textile weavers) 23
banners 13, 14; bags for 11, 166, *101*
Barbarigo, Daniele 29
Başkent 8
Bāyazīd I (Sultan) 34
Bāyazīd II (Sultan) 12, 20, 21, 32, 34, 35, 43, *3, 4, 6, 18*; Treasury inventory (1505) 13, 27, 28, 39, 159, 165
Bāyazīd (Şehzāde; prince) 12, 28, 33, *18*
bedspreads 160, 162, 166, *97, 110*
Belgrade 13
Bellini, Jacopo 23
Bethlen, Prince Gabriel 160, 163
books and bookbinding 163, 164–5, *95*
bohça (wrapper) 11–12, 160, 162, 165, 166, *96, 100, 103, 104*
Bolghary 43; leather 42
bolster-covers 159, 160, 162, 166, *111*
Borlandi, Francesco 31
Boston, Mass.: Museum of Fine Arts 155 (*54*)
bow-cases 162, 164, *92*
brocades (*çātma*; *kemha*) 15–16, 18, 19; use in garments *1, 14, 23, 27, 28, 30, 31, 33, 34, 38, 42, 43, 45–7, 49*
Bronzino (painter) 33

Bursa 7, 8, 32, 33, 163; edict (of 1502) 20, 21, 22; shawls 40; silks 14, 16, 29; velvets 16
Busbecq, Ogier Ghiselin de 18, 40
Byzantium 7, 35

Cairo 13, 31, 32
Çaldıran 8, 42
Cem Sultan (prince) 13
Charles V (Emperor) 13, 40
chinoiserie 164, 165, *78, 93*
Chios 15, 17
cloth of gold/silver, *see* lamé
coats, cloaks and jackets *73, 80–3, 85*
coffee service 167; case for pot 166, *109*; cloth for *115, 116*
Colbert, Jean Baptiste 20, 23
Constantinople 7–8, 34; *see also* Istanbul
Contarini, Bartolo 37
Contarini, Tomà 162
Corneille, Pierre 26
Crimea 42
curtains and hangings 159, 160, 162, 167
cushion-covers 162; *see also* bolster-covers

Damascus 17
Diyarbekir 12
Dresden: Museum für Kunsthandwerk 154 (*42*)
dresses (women's) 166, *67, 68*; *see also* robes and gowns
dyes 18–19, 29

Edirne 7, 20, 21, 163; furriers 43
Egypt 7, 8, 12, 13, 18, 27, 31, 38, 42, 164
embroideries 8, 159–67, *63, 64, 86–121*
England: woollen exports 39

Faṭma Sulṭān *60–6*
floor-coverings 159–60
Florence 27; weaving 21, 23, (satins) 17, (woollens) 39; Uffizi 33
France: satins 17; silk factories 209; (Lyons silk) 16, 27, 209 (*105*); woollen exports 39
Franceschi, Domenico de 33
furs: trade 42–5; use of 20, *3, 63*

Galata (Pera) 39, 44, 160, 164
Galland, Antoine 26, 28, 40
Gelibolulu Musṭafā Paşa 164, *95*
Genoa 21, 23
George I Rakóczy 160, 161, 166
Gevher Sulṭān *96*

al-Ghawrī (Mamlūk Sultan) 13, 16
gold thread, uses of: *see* lamé, metal thread
guilds 21
Gustavus Adolphus (of Sweden) 166

Habsburg embassies 32, 33
handkerchiefs, embroidered 159, 160, 163, 164, *88, 90, 91*
Ḥānzāde Sulṭān *36*
Ḥaydār Reīs 32
head-bands 159, 164, *89*
head-covers 159
Herberstein, Siegmund von 33
Hijaz 13, 18
Hungary 160, 162
Hüseyin Ağa 44

Ibn Baṭṭuṭa 12
Ibn Iyās (historian) 13, 38
Ibrāhīm (Sultan) 43, *22, 47*
Ibrāhīm Paşa (vizier) 22, 37
India 8, 18
inks 19
interior decoration 159, 161, 162, 167
Iran 7, 8, 15; Safavid 42; silks 16
Ismāʿīl (Shah) 160
Istanbul 7–8, 16, 22–3, 33, 159; furriers 43; looms 16; Military Museum 13; *see also* Galata, price registers, Topkapı Saray Museum
Italy 8, 18, 19, 21–2, 23, 32–3; fabric designs *28, 27, 28, 43, 46*, (silks) 34, (velvet) 160; woollen trade 32, 39; *see also* Florence, Venice
Iznik 28–9

Janissaries 39, 156 (*74*)
Justinian (Byzantine emperor) 39

Kaffa 34, 42
kaftans 12, 25, 27–8, *1–11, 13–25, 27–35, 38–56, 58–60, 74, 76, 78, 79*; embroidered *86, 87*; *see also* robes of honour
Kashmir 40–1
Ḳāsim (Şehzāde) *35, 37*
Ḳāsim (Hungarian embroiderer) 160, 163
Kayqubād I and II 34
kiswa (veil) 11–12, 13
Konya 34
Korans 19
Kraków 13
Krefeld: Gewebesammlung 153 (*28*), 154 (*46*), 156 (*76*)

lace 164
Lahore 40
lamé (*seraser*; cloth of gold/silver) 15–16, 17, 37, 161; garments *9, 14, 21, 32, 39, 42, 46, 48, 50, 51, 54, 58, 61, 64, 72, 76*; *see also* metal thread
leather, embroidered 163, 165, 166, *93, 94, 109*
Leningrad 34
Levnī (painter) 27
linen, embroidered *91, 96, 97, 99, 118, 119*
Louis XIV (of France) 20
Lyons: silk 16, 27, 209 (105); Musée Historique de Tissus 34, 153 (*27*), 154 (*34, 46*), 155 (*49*), 156 (*70*)

Maḥmūd I (Sultan) 11, 16, 162, *55–7*
Maḥmud II (Sultan) 14, *77–9*
Mamlūks 14, 31, 38, 42
Manisa 12
Maria (of Mangop) 34
Maringhi, Giovanni de Francesco 39
mats (*nihālī*) 165, 166, *105, 108*
Mecca 7; Ka'ba at 12
Medina 7
Meḥmed II (the Conqueror; Sultan) 7, 11, 28, 34, 35, 42, *1, 2, 48*
Meḥmed III (Sultan) 11, 20, *27, 28, 48*
Meḥmed IV (Sultan) *48, 49*
Meḥmed V Reşād (Sultan) *85*
Meḥmed (Şehzāde) 164, *86–8, 98*
Mesopotamia 8
metal thread and braid (gold/silver) 159–60, 161, 166–7, *1, 19, 23, 47, 58, 62, 63, 65–9, 71, 73, 79–83, 85–95, 105–7, 109, 110, 112–16, 118, 120, 121*; *see also* lamé
Mocenigo, Alvise 37
Mocenigo, Tomà 13
Mohács, Battle of 165
mohair 39–40
Moldavia 33, 34
Montagu, Lady Mary Wortley 26, 27, 162–3
Moscow 42; Kremlin 29, 34
Mosul 32
Mour, Jean Baptiste Van 163
Muḥammad 'Alī 26
Muḥammad Sulṭān 12
Murād II (Sultan) 11
Murād III (Sultan) 11, 12, 19, 164, *21, 23–6*
Murād IV (Sultan) 11, *41, 43–6*
Murād V (Sultan) *83*
Muscovy 29, 33, 42–3
muslin, embroidered *88, 90*
Muṣṭafā II (Sultan) 11, 48
Muṣṭafā III (Sultan) 11–12, 26, *58, 59*
Muṣṭafā IV (Sultan) *76*
Muṣṭafā (Şehzāde) 33, *18*

Nādir Shāh 162
nakkaşhane (Court studio) 22, 23, 163
napkins 160, 166, *99, 119*
Naṣīr al-Dīn Ṭūsī 35
Nicolay, Nicolas de 33
Nigārī (painter), see Ḥaydār Reīs
Nüsretnāme (Gelibolulu Muṣṭafā Alī) 164, *95*

Ohsson, Mouradjea d' 26, 27, 41, 44
'Osmān I (Sultan) 11
'Osmān II (Sultan) 11, *38–40, 42*
Ottomans 7–8, 11; Court workshops 20, 22–3, 163; decrees and edicts (use of furs) 43, (looms) 16, (taxes on mohair) 40, (silver) 160; dyes 18–19; fur trade 42–5; inventories 15, 162, (of Bāyazīd II) 12, 18, 20, 27, 28, 43, 159, 165; registers of clothing 11–12; registers of craftsmen 160; price registers 16, 17, 20, 39, 40, 43; silk industry 15–17, 20–4, (patterns) 28–9
over-garments (*ḥırḳa*) *12, 37*; (*üstlük*) 163, *120, 121*; *see also* coats, cloaks and jackets

Pagan, Mathio 164
Palestine 32
pattern books 164
Pegolotti, Balduccio 31
Persia, *see* Iran
Pisanello 23
Poland 33; fur trade 42
Pollaiuolo, Antonio 23
Polo, Marco 31–2
Prato: Archivio Datini 32
prayer mats (*seccāde*) 165–6, *102, 106, 112*

Qā'ītbāy (Sultan) 13
quivers 160, 161

Rifā'a Rāfi' al-Ṭaḥtawī 26
robes and gowns *26, 36, 57, 61, 62, 64–6, 69, 70, 72, 75, 77*; Thracian *120, 121*
robes of honour 14, 21, 27, 28, 42
Romania 34
Roseto (Giovanventuro Roseti) 18
Roxelane 164, *89, 90*
Rudolf II (Habsburg) 28, 162, 165
Rukīye Sulṭān (princess) *72*
Russia, *see* Muscovy
Rustam (hero) 164

saddle-cloths 161, 162, 166
Safavids 15, 160; painting 163
Sāliḥa Sulṭān (daughter of Abdü'l-Hamīd) *67–70*
Sāliḥa Sulṭān (daughter of Meḥmed III) 167
Samarkand 12
Sanuto, Marino 16, 25–6, 28, 32, 38, 162
Saruhan 12
sashes, embroidered 166, *117*
satins 16, 17; garments *4–8, 10, 15–17, 21, 22, 35, 36, 44, 51, 53, 56, 75*; embroidered *100, 103–5, 110, 114–16*
Selīm I (the Grim; Sultan) 7, 11, 16, 27, 28, 32, 37, 42, *5, 7–12*
Selīm II (Sultan) 11, 32, *19, 20*
Selīm III (Sultan) 14, 39, 44, *74, 75*
Seljuks 34
seraser, *see* lamé
Serbia 34
Seyyid Loqmān 32
Shāh Rukh 12
shawls 40–1
silk 15–17, 20–4, 27; embroideries *88–108, 119*; garments *12, 13, 18–20, 23, 25, 26, 29, 33, 37, 40, 41, 52, 57, 59, 60, 62, 65–71, 75, 77–9*; *see also* brocades, satin, velvet, etc.
silver thread, uses of, *see* lamé, metal thread and braid
Sinai 32
Skokloster (Sweden) 165
slave labour 22, 42
Spain 18, 19; fabric designs *43, 45*, 155 (*49*); merino wool 39
spice trade 31
Stockholm 34, 165
Süleymān II (the Magnificent; Sultan) 11, 16, 26, 160, 164; dress 37, 40, *13–17*; portraits of 33
Süleymān III (Sultan) *50, 51*
Syria 7, 8

tablecloths *105, 114*
Tabriz 42
taffeta 15
Tamerlane 12
tapestries 13
Tavernier, Jean Baptiste 13, 161
tents 13; tent-work 162
Thrace 39, 162, 163; woman's over-gown *120, 121*
throne-cloths 161
tile patterns 28–9
Tīmūr, *see* Tamerlane
Tintoretto 28
Titian 33
tomb furnishings 12
Topkapı Saray Museum/Palace 7–8, 11; Arz Odası (Audience Chamber) 161, 162; Hazine (Treasury) 7, 11, 159; Hırka-i Saadet Dairesi 7, 12; Library 23; Sünnet Odası (Circumcision Room) 28, 48
towels 159, 160, 166, *107, 118*
Transcaucasia 11, 19
Transylvania 33, 160, 162
Trevisan (Venetian ambassador) 13
Tripoli (Lebanon) 16
Tunisia 19
turbans 26; turban-covers 159, 165, *98*

'ulamā' 25, 26, 39
al-'Umarī 38

velvet 15, 16, *1–3, 11, 24, 27, 28, 31, 42, 43, 49, 55, 72*; embroidered *92, 101, 120*
Venice 27, 28, 29, 32, 33; Museo Correr 14; and Egypt 38; merchants from 160; satins from 16, 17; textile designs 164, *31*
Ventura, Pagnini della 31
Vicenza 37
Vienna 13, 14, 34

Wallachia 33
Walters Art Gallery, Baltimore 168 (*93*)
wool and woollen fabrics 39–41, *74, 80–5*; embroidered *106, 113, 121*
Wrangel, Carl Gustav 165
wrappers, *see bohça*

Yazd 15
yazılı gömlek (talismanic shirts) 13